We Reach the Moon

We
Reach the Moon

Young Readers' Edition

A *New York Times* Book
by JOHN NOBLE WILFORD

Based upon the original book published by
𝕿𝖍𝖊 𝕹𝖊𝖜 𝖄𝖔𝖗𝖐 𝕿𝖎𝖒𝖊𝖘 *and Bantam Books*

A W. W. NORTON BOOK
Published by
GROSSET & DUNLAP, INC.
New York

Grateful acknowledgement is made for permission to reprint the following copyrighted material:

Narrative by Robert Jastrow appearing in Chapter 14 © 1969 by The New York Times Company. Reprinted by permission.

Photographs courtesy of NASA

Acknowledgments

This is, first and foremost, a newspaper reporter's book. I am not a scientist or engineer. But my years of covering the Apollo Project were an enlightening adult-education course in the fields of knowledge I either neglected as a university student or was not even exposed to in the pre-space curriculum. Nor am I a certified historian. But no journalist who looks beyond his typewriter can ignore the elements of history in the raw material that is his story.

And I am not—I was about to say, I am not a romantic, a dreamer, for journalists pride themselves on being detached observers of other men's passions. But who could cover the story of man's first footsteps on another world, and cover it as more than science story or another nuts-and-bolts technology story, without feeling in himself a flutter of all the romantic urges that have sent men across oceans, up mountains, and out into the air and then the space beyond the air? I could not.

Whatever future historians may say of Apollo, I will be grateful to *The New York Times* for the opportunity to be a close observer of this great adventure.

This is not solely my book. I owe a large debt to a number of members of the *Times* staff, including Walter Sullivan, Henry R. Lieberman, Richard Witkin, Harold M. Schmeck, Jr., Sandra Blakeslee, and Douglas Kneeland. Their stories and editorial assistance were an invaluable contribution to the book. The diagrams are the work of the *Times* map department, headed by Andrew Sabbatini.

I want to single out for credit Richard D. Lyons, a boon companion and especially helpful colleague through all the major Apollo missions, and William K. Stevens, who provided most of the material and writing for the chapter on the Apollo 11 crew. Another good companion and colleague through all this was Douglas M. Dederer, who was especially helpful during my many visits to Cape Kennedy. The National Aeronautics and Space Administration and many of the major Apollo industrial contractors helped make available the many documents and background materials that facilitated coverage of Apollo.

Others who made the book possible were Carter Horsley and Sydnor Vanderschmidt, who made important research contributions. Mark Bloom was kind enough to read and offer suggestions on a part of the book. Mary Rourke typed much of the manuscript.

No one gave me more encouragement than my wife, Nancy, who shares my enthusiasm for the story and was uncomplaining of the time taken from our lives by the program to get men to the moon.

Every writer needs an editor, and I was fortunate to have two very skillful and understanding editors—Lee Foster and Donald Johnston. Michael A. Chester was the able editor of this particular edition of the book. Finally, I want to thank Jack Stewart, who had the original idea, for his encouragement and patience over the long months of giving birth to this book.

JNW
October 1969

To Nona and Susan

Contents

We Reach the Moon

CHAPTER 1

Footprints on the Moon

On the lonely, lifeless landscape of the moon, a strange-looking vehicle squats motionless under the sun's glaring rays. On one of its four spindly legs is attached a small, stainless steel plaque which reads:

HERE MEN FROM THE PLANET EARTH

FIRST SET FOOT UPON THE MOON.

JULY 1969 A.D.

WE CAME IN PEACE FOR ALL MANKIND.

The vehicle, the cast-off lower half of a lunar landing craft, is a monument to the historic event on July 20, when two American astronauts planted the first human footsteps on the moon.

The monument will stay there for ages, for there is no wind or water on the moon to wear it away.

The man who took the first step was Neil A. Armstrong, the 38-year-old civilian commander of the Apollo 11. As he reached the bottom of the landing craft's ladder and extended his booted left foot to touch the moon's powdery surface, he said: "That's one small step for a man, one giant leap for mankind."

He was followed down the ladder minutes later by Edwin E. Aldrin, Jr., a 39-year-old Air Force colonel. For 2 hours and 21 minutes, the two men, carefully at first and then boldly, wandered about on the barren, rock-strewn surface. They tested their ability to move about on this strange world. They took photographs of the landscape. They set up scientific experiments and collected rock and soil samples. They set up a television camera so the whole world could watch. At one point, Armstrong said to Aldrin, "Isn't this fun?"

All the while, the third member of the crew, Michael Collins, 38, an Air Force lieutenant colonel, piloted the Command Ship in lunar orbit 70 miles above the surface, waiting for the two explorers to rejoin him for the trip back to earth. Altogether, the visit to the moon lasted 21 hours and 37 minutes.

AN INCREDIBLE TRIUMPH

For the Apollo 11 crew, and for the United States space team, the successful 500,000-mile mission involving 88 separate steps was an incredible triumph of skill and courage. For the world, it was the most dramatic proof of what man can do if he puts his mind to it. The moon, which used to seem unreachable, was now within man's reach, the first port of call in the new age of spacefaring.

There have been other daring expeditions, of course. But

Apollo 11 was different: the world watched it as it happened. Through television and radio, hundreds of millions of people followed the activities aboard Columbia, the command ship, and Eagle, the landing craft—names chosen because, as Armstrong put it, they were "representative of the flight and the nation's hope." The television pictures across the 238,000 miles from the moon were so clear and sharp, showing the deep shadows and bright sunlight, that they seemed almost unreal.

Though the mission was completed almost without flaw, it was filled with suspense and anxiety. The astronauts faced risks on the moon never before met by man. And, as with all space flights, chances of failure and disaster were ever present—the blast-off of the giant Saturn 5 rocket at Cape Kennedy, the entry of the spaceship into earth and lunar orbits, the never-before-attempted landing and lift-off from the moon, the link-up of Columbia and Eagle, the re-entry into the atmosphere, the splashdown. An error or failure of any of the millions of individual parts anywhere along the way could have ended the mission short of the goal. An equipment failure or accident on the moon could have left the astronauts stranded.

HEROES

But they made it. After eight days in space, they splashed down in the Pacific to a presidential greeting aboard the recovery carrier, the U.S.S. Hornet. They were the heroes of the nation and the world.

"This is the greatest week in the history of the world since the Creation," President Nixon told the space travelers. "As a result of what you've done, the world has never been closer together before."

The welcome was not the familiar red-carpet ceremony of

space missions in which the returning astronauts walk across the deck of the carrier. The Apollo 11 crewmen were inside an isolation van and they talked with Mr. Nixon by microphone. The astronauts were under quarantine because of the slim chance that they brought back some deadly moon virus for which man has no immunity.

People everywhere were excited by this moon trip. Perhaps never before had one event so captured the world's imagination and spirit of adventure. There were some grumbles about problems to be solved here on earth, but for days Apollo was all over the headlines, TV sets, and radios throughout the world.

What moved the human spirit was, as Aldrin put it in a thoughtful moment on the way home, the "curiosity of all mankind to explore the unknown" that had sent explorers to brave the harshest conditions of this planet—to the poles, to the tops of mountains, to the loftiest balloon altitudes, to the deepest portions of the sea. Then why not the moon?

There were critics who said that the Apollo program cost too much, that the money and talent could be more usefully directed to fighting disease and poverty, that it was a "childish stunt" to make a race out of going to the moon. But by the time of the moon trip, many people began to think that the astronauts might bring back some clues to help solve the mysteries of the universe.

Whatever would be learned from the Apollo 11 voyage, it was a great expansion for mankind. It was a journey that took man beyond the earth to walk on another world.

CHAPTER 2

The Target

By the time the Apollo 11 astronauts began preparing for their lunar voyage, scientists had gathered enormous amounts of data about the moon. For thousands of years astronomers have been looking at the moon, studying its appearance and its motion through the sky. For the past 360 years, detailed views of the moon have been made possible through the use of telescopes. More recently, we have been able to reflect radar signals from the moon and to send scientific instruments to the moon on unmanned rockets. Radar signals and rockets able to travel through outer space are the products of our fast-moving scientific age, and they have shown us things about the moon that could never have been known before.

What, then, was known about the moon as the Apollo astronauts set out for their landing? What sort of world were they going to visit?

One way to picture the earth and the moon is to think of them as a pair of dancing partners spinning wildly around a dance floor with the sun in the center. Since the earth is 81 times as heavy as the moon, it is the anchor man in the dance.

Instead of keeping the same face toward its little dancing partner all the time, the earth spins like a top. This spin turns all parts of the earth toward the moon. The same spin also turns all parts of the earth toward the sun, giving us our day and night. A single spin of the earth takes about 24 hours—actually 23 hours and 56 minutes.

The moon spins much more slowly than the earth—so slowly that it always keeps the same face toward the earth. It makes one complete spin in the same amount of time that it takes to make a complete orbit around the earth. The time that the moon takes for a single orbit and a single spin is $27\frac{1}{3}$ days. This period of time has an old name—it is called a "month."

Astronomers have a down-to-earth way of illustrating the moon's motions. Stand in a room, they suggest, and place a chair in front of you. You are the moon; the chair is the earth. First, go all the way around the chair, always facing the same wall. That is *not* the way the moon moves, because you "orbited" but you did not spin. Now, go around the chair, facing the chair at all times. You will find that you orbited once around the chair, *and* you spun once. The same part of your body was always facing the chair. So it is with the moon and earth.

The way the moon always keeps its same side toward the earth comes about because the gravitational pull of the earth controls the motions of the moon. Each of the bodies is constantly affected by the other's presence. The tidal forces between the two, for instance, are unmatched elsewhere in the solar system. The moon's gravitational force causes earth's oceans to rise and fall and that is why we have high and low tides. Also, the earth's constant tugging has caused a definite bulge on the side of the moon that faces the earth. The earth is not a perfect ball either, but is a little bit pear shaped, and the moon's pull has partly caused that.

Other planets in the solar system have their moons, too. Jupiter, the largest of the nine planets, has twelve moons orbiting around it. The smallest of these is only 14 miles in diameter, and the largest is Ganymede, 3100 miles in diameter, the largest moon in the solar system. Saturn has ten moons, in addition to its amazing rings. The largest of Saturn's moons is Titan, 3,000 miles in diameter. Uranus has five moons, Neptune and Mars have two moons each, and Mercury and Venus have none. If far-away Pluto has any moons, they have not yet been observed. In fact, many astronomers think that Pluto may once have been a moon of Neptune until it escaped into its own orbit around the sun.

The earth-moon system is unusual, though, because the earth (with a diameter of 7,963 miles) is a comparatively small planet, while our moon (with a diameter of 2,160 miles) is a comparatively large moon. Therefore, astronomers often think of the earth-moon system as a double planet. This double planet, making a full orbit around the sun once every 365 days, may be one of the most beautiful systems in the universe. Of course, we cannot know that for certain, because we are not yet able to travel to another sun and see its family of planets. But we did take a step in that direction when the Apollo astronauts landed on the moon.

The moon has no detectable atmosphere—neither air nor any other gases. Therefore, it has no weather—no wind, no clouds, no rain, no snow, no water on the surface. People obviously have to take along their own air and water.

The moon's lack of atmosphere causes strange effects. Except for the voices and cracklings on their built-in radio sets and the sounds of their own breathing and motions, the astronauts hear nothing, because there is no air to carry sound waves. Also, there is no color in the moon's sky—only blackness, both day and night. (The blue of earth's sky is caused by particles of air scattering the sunlight.) By day a brilliant sun lights the surface of the moon. By day and night, stars shine in the black sky much more brightly than they do in our night sky. Stars seen from the moon do not twinkle—the twinkling that we are used to is caused by the star-light passing through the air.

Looking up from the moon's surface, the Apollo astronauts were able to see the great, shining earth. Since the earth is larger than the moon and a better reflector of sunlight, earthshine on the moon is more than eight times as bright as moonshine on the earth. If the astronauts had been on the moon for an entire month, they would have seen the earth go through different phases— crescent earth, half earth, and full earth. The phase of the earth (like the phase of the moon when we look at it) would depend on the direction that the sunlight was coming from and what portion of the sunlit part of the earth was visible at any time.

The earth's atmosphere protects people in many ways. Astronauts on the moon have to do without that protection. For instance, with no air to filter out some of the sun's heat, the surface of the moon is heated to a temperature of about 260 degrees Fahrenheit. Just how hot that is can be seen from the fact that water boils at the earth's surface at 212 degrees Fahrenheit. During the lunar night the temperature plunges to at least 240 degrees below zero Fahrenheit—low enough to freeze the mercury in a thermometer. That is because the moon does not have an atmosphere to act as a blanket, to hold much of the day's heat when the sun goes down. Visitors to the moon must also remember that, because of the moon's slower spin, lunar days and nights each last about two weeks of earth time.

In addition to light, there are dangerous radiations given off by the sun. These rays are made up of atomic-sized particles that do not reach earth because of the shielding air. But these rays do bombard the moon. A sudden flare-up of this radiation could be very dangerous to astronauts and they would have to take cover inside a shielded spacecraft or inside caves or other shelters on the moon.

Scientists are not sure whether the moon ever did have an atmosphere. If the moon did have an atmosphere billions of years ago, its weak gravity could not hold onto the gases and let them slip away into space. The moon's surface gravity is only about one-sixth as strong as earth's surface gravity.

The moon's low gravity has its advantages. For one thing, it would be easier to launch a rocket off the moon than off the earth. The moon's grip on objects is not as strong as earth's. This makes it possible for astronauts on the moon to lift heavier objects and take longer, springier steps than they could on earth. A person or object weighing 180 pounds on earth would weigh only 30 pounds on the moon. An astronaut would be able to leap 20 feet off the ground.

However, there is another kind of heaviness called "inertia" that has nothing to do with gravitational pull. The heavier an object is, the harder it is to stop it or make it turn once it is in motion, and the harder it is to start it moving when it is still. It is inertia that makes a big truck harder to stop, or turn, or get moving again, compared with stopping, turning, or pulling away from a stop in a small sports car.

Even though the *weight* of a person or an object on the moon would be much less, making enormous leaps and the lifting of very heavy objects possible, *inertia* would not change. An object on the moon would have just as much inertia as it would on earth. So, an astronaut making great leaps and bounds across the moon would find that it would be hard to turn or dodge or come to a stop. The result could be a dangerous crashing against things that might damage his spacesuit or break his bones. Therefore, astronauts on the moon do not make the great leaps that they could make.

THE LANDSCAPE OF THE MOON

When you look at the sunlit surface of the moon, you can see that there are both light and dark patches. It is the pattern of dark patches on the bright moon that people have seen as the outlines of an imaginary face—"the man in the moon."

Telescope studies of the moon show that the brighter areas are mountains and rugged highlands. The dark patches are smoother plains. The early astronomers thought that these plains were seas. They gave them such names as "Sea of Showers," "Sea of Clouds," and "Ocean of Storms." These names are still used, even though the so-called seas are now known to be dry, flat stretches of land.

Scientists have suggested various theories to explain how these great plains were formed on the moon. One theory is that they are great areas of dust caused by meteorites and dust particles striking the moon for billions of years—and some scientists thought that these dust layers were so deep and loose that they might swallow up anyone who landed there.

Another theory is that these plains were formed as spreading pools of molten lava. According to this theory, a large meteor hitting the moon would melt the surface rock by the force of the collision. The melted rock would flow, as lava, across the landscape, covering old craters and all but the highest peaks. Another possible source of the lava might have been the eruption of a volcano.

Still another theory is that these plains are dark areas because they are covered with the leftovers of plant life that might have existed on the moon billions of years ago. Dr. John J. Gilvarry of the National Aeronautics and Space Administration (NASA) originated this theory. He believed that the moon had true seas when it was young, but that they evaporated into mist, which drifted away into space because of the moon's weak gravity. But the seas might have been there long enough for life to develop. After the seas were gone, layers of this living material may have been left behind.

Scientists also have different theories about the lunar craters, the most striking features of the moon's surface.

Thousands of craters, ranging in diameter from the 160-mile-wide Clavius down to those no bigger across than a silver dollar, give the moon its scarred appearance. A person standing at the center of one of the broader craters would be unable to see the crater walls. That is because the moon, being smaller than earth, has a surface that curves more sharply.

Some of the craters are amazingly deep. The crater Newton is so deep (29,000 feet) that Mount Everest would barely peep out the top if it were set down there. No sunlight or earthshine ever casts a cheery ray on the dark floor of Newton. A number of craters, such as the 75-mile-wide Alphonsus, are a puzzle to astronomers because of the mountain peaks rising from their floors. These peaks are usually found near the centers of the craters and never seem to be as high as the surrounding walls. There are even craters within craters, as in the case of the central crater of the large crater Copernicus, the so-called "monarch of the moon." Typical of many "young" craters is Tycho Brahe, a 56-mile-wide depression in the south of the moon. Rays of very light materials stretch out from its rim, some for 1,000 miles. These rays seem to be the marks of the birth of the crater, and they are probably the splash marks left when dirt and rocks were flung outward. This sunburst effect makes Tycho one of the most brilliant sights on the moon.

Many scientists believe that lunar craters were formed by the collisions of meteors and comets against the moon. However, the case is not closed, and some scientists argue that the craters came from volcanic eruptions.

Other features of the landscape include the highlands and mountains, rills and ridges, deep faults and long valleys.

In the highlands, believed to be the oldest parts of the moon's surface, there are so many craters that they overlap. The broken fragments of crater walls seem to have piled up to form the surrounding rough landscape, and some of the ridges are thought to be leftover walls of old craters. From the edges of the plains, chains of mountains rise up. The largest, the Leibniz range, which lies near the south pole, has peaks up to 30,000 feet tall.

The rills of the moon, another common feature, are streaks or cracks that look like streams. They may have once been "river beds" for streams of red-hot lava. Deeper breaks or faults have also been seen. They may be a sign that the moon has violent "moonquakes" just as the earth has earthquakes.

Though it is popular to speak of the moon as a dead world, an orbiting cinder, scientists are not so sure. In 1956, a Russian astronomer, Nikolai A. Kozyrev, detected what seemed to be traces of gas flowing out of the crater Aristarchus. Two years later, his instruments showed a possible gas release from the crater Alphonsus. These observations show that there may be some active stirring just beneath the quiet-looking surface of the moon.

The scientific data brought back by the Apollo astronauts should help to solve many of these mysteries about the moon. By the time the data has been carefully studied, scientists may also know more about the birth of the moon. This question has been an important one in our century—where did the moon come from?

There are three theories about the birth of the moon. In the first, the moon is thought to have formed somewhere in space, after which it wandered until captured by the earth's gravitational field. The second theory is that the moon was once part of earth, then split off and went into orbit. In the third theory, the moon is believed to have developed as a separate body at the same time as earth, perhaps from materials left over from the formation of earth. But, whatever the birth of the moon was like, most scientists agree that the moon became a satellite of the earth soon after the two bodies were formed. That would make the moon about $4\frac{1}{2}$ billion years old.

However the moon was formed, the fact that men would soon be able to visit it built up new scientific interest in earth's nearest neighbor. To many astronomers, the moon had seemed to be a dull, unchanging world compared with Mars or Jupiter or the distant stars. But the Apollo project changed that. People began to see the moon as a place for great discoveries. As the Nobel prizewinning scientist Harold C. Urey pointed out, the very slowly changing surface of the moon makes it a place where the marks of events billions of years old may still be seen. In that way, the moon is like a window into the very distant past. Robert Jastrow of NASA's Goddard Space Institute put it this way: "Because its surface has preserved the record of ancient events, it holds a key to the history of the solar system."

In the summer of 1965, a group of leading scientists from the National Academy of Sciences met at Woods Hole on Cape Cod, a place where men usually spend their time exploring the inner space of the oceans. The scientists were meeting to consider what the first men on the moon should do to gather as much valuable scientific information as they could in a short time. The scientists were interested in finding out many different things about the moon. They hoped that the astronauts would bring back information about the kinds of rock that the moon is made of, the causes of craters, the age of the moon, traces of volcanic activity, the number of meteors hitting the moon, measurements of radiation striking the moon from the sun and from outer space, and any traces of magnetism in the moon rocks.

Not all of the questions could be answered on the first landing, to be sure, but the instruments to be carried to the moon should be designed to find out as much as possible. The suggestions included an instrument to detect any tremors in the moon's surface, either from a moonquake, a volcanic eruption, or a meteor impact. The scientists also wanted the astronauts to bring back as many samples of lunar soil as possible. They also suggested an experiment to collect any gases spewed out by the sun to bombard the moon. They had other, more complicated suggestions, but NASA finally decided that setting up a quake detector, collecting rocks, and laying out a gas detector and other instruments would occupy enough of the time and energy of the first men on the moon.

With these scientific goals in mind, the United States began preparing a fleet of unmanned picture-taking spacecraft to scout out the moon in advance of the men of Apollo. These were the Ranger crash-landers, Surveyor soft-landers, and Lunar Orbiters (see Chapter 4). Besides sending back a wealth of intriguing scientific data, these robots would reassure Apollo planners that they knew how to get to the moon.

CHAPTER 3

Charting the Way to the Moon

In 1961, under the leadership of President Kennedy, the decision to build the Apollo moonship was made. It was clear, at that time, that the problem of how to build such a moonship was not going to be easily solved.

In the months following the Kennedy decision, five plans were being considered for the Apollo design. At first, the most popular method was "direct ascent." It seemed to be the simplest. A monster, three-stage rocket would blast a spaceship weighing about 150,000 pounds across space toward the moon. When it neared the moon, the spaceship would go into an orbit around the moon. Then, the ship's retro-rockets would fire.

The retro-rockets of an orbiting spaceship act as brakes. For a ship nose-first in orbit, the blasting retro-rockets, if aimed toward the line of flight, would send their flaming gases out in a forward direction, causing a backward push on the ship. This backward push would make the ship lose orbit energy and begin to spiral downward. For the moonship orbiting around the moon, the retro-blast would send it down toward the surface of the moon.

After the crew explored the moon, they would blast off in their spaceship and head back to earth.

This whole approach to visiting the moon had the advantage of being very simple and direct. But there was a disadvantage— an enormous amount of rocket power would be needed to do the job. The *direct-ascent* method would mean building a rocket nearly twice as powerful as the most powerful rockets in the world. It would be named the "Nova," and its rocket thrust at blast-off would be an enormous force measuring 13 million pounds.

But, it would be many years before the Nova could be built and tested. Besides, at that time, nobody was sure that the moon's crust would be strong enough to support the weight of the big 150,000-pound spaceship that the Nova would send to the moon. There was also a chance that such a tall ship (80 to 100 feet) might topple over when it made its moon landing. One NASA engineer said it would be almost like trying to land the Washington Monument on its base.

So, turning away from this simple, "brute force" approach, the designers began to think about a plan called "earth-orbit rendezvous." The American rocket specialist Wernher von Braun, who had come to this country from Germany to play an important part in space research, originally favored this method. Rather than launching the entire spaceship with a big Nova-type booster, smaller rockets would launch parts of the moonship. Perhaps five different sections of the moonship would be launched separately into orbit around the earth. Astronauts working in outer space would connect the orbiting sections to complete the building of the moonship.

While the *earth-orbit rendezvous* would do away with any need for the Nova rocket, it still left problems. The weight of the moonship, once it was put together in its earth orbit, would be about the same as it would be in the brute-force plan. So, the moon landing would be just as hard to do. Another problem was the split-second timing needed for the five separate launchings, in order for the sections of the moonship to come together for their orbital meeting or "rendezvous."

A different kind of rendezvous called the "tanker" method began to get a lot of scientific attention. The idea called for sending an unmanned tanker rocket into earth orbit. Then, the Apollo moonship would be sent into orbit by a Saturn 5 booster. The Apollo would use the tanker as an "orbital service station," docking at the tanker and getting filled with rocket fuel. Then it would separate from the tanker and rocket toward the moon. The advantage of this method would be that all the extra fuel supplied by the tanker would not have to be boosted from the launch pad with the moonship. It was one more way to use smaller boosters and stay away from the enormous Nova rocket. But fueling in orbit, especially using the super-cold liquid oxygen, seemed to be a complicated and risky operation.

A fourth possibility was "lunar-surface rendezvous." Extra fuel and supplies would be rocketed to the moon's surface on board unmanned spaceships. After the astronauts landed from a direct flight, they could refuel from the supplies that were waiting for them on the moon before they started their return flight to earth. But there would be serious risks. First, there would be no way of knowing if the supplies had landed without damage. There was the added risk that the astronauts might land too far from the supplies and would be unable to refuel. That would leave them stranded on the moon.

While scientists and government leaders were trying to decide among these four plans, a NASA engineer named John C. Houbolt suggested a fifth plan. His plan became known as "lunar-orbit rendezvous." According to this plan, a Saturn 5 rocket, launched from the earth, would boost the Apollo ship toward the moon, with a crew of three astronauts. Apollo would go into orbit around the moon. But the entire moonship would not land on the moon. Instead, a small landing craft would be separated from the moonship. The landing craft, carrying two astronauts, would use its retro-rocket to reach the moon's surface. The third astronaut would stay on board the main part of the moonship, orbiting around the moon while his crewmates explored the surface. When the exploration was completed, the two astronauts on the moon would blast off in the landing craft to join the moonship once more. Then, leaving the landing craft to orbit around the moon as an empty shell, the three astronauts would rocket back toward earth in the main part of the Apollo moonship.

The lunar lander would do for Apollo what a small boat does for a big ship. Rather than land a big ship on a shallow shore, it is more practical to anchor the ship offshore and use a boat to land on the beach. The same sort of idea fitted the *lunar-orbit rendezvous*. It would take a lot of rocket energy and fuel weight to land Apollo on the moon and then to blast off again from the moon's surface. By parking the Apollo in orbit and using the small landing craft, the landing could be carried out with a much smaller cost in rocket fuel. More weight would be saved by leaving the landing craft in orbit around the moon instead of having to carry its weight on the trip back.

Many Apollo planners thought that the lunar-orbit rendezvous was too risky. They were worried about the idea of the astronauts having to carry out the exact rendezvous maneuvers 230,000 miles from earth. Would it not be less risky, they asked, to try for rendezvous in earth orbit where, if anything went wrong, it would be easier to bring the men back to earth? Also, some scientists felt that the small landing craft would not be able to carry enough instruments for a thorough study of the moon's surface.

But, after much argument and study, it was decided that the lunar-orbit rendezvous had so many advantages that it was undoubtedly the best of the five methods. Its lower cost, the fact that it could be built in time for a moon trip in the late 1960's, and the fact that it was fairly simple to develop made it the best all-around choice.

Out of the smoke of battle came the first clear outline of how the United States would try to meet President Kennedy's pledge to reach the moon in the 1960's. Lunar-orbit rendezvous would be used. The booster at the launch pad would be a three-stage Saturn 5 rocket, with a thrust of $7\frac{1}{2}$ million pounds at lift-off. As each rocket stage used up all its fuel and burned out, it would be dropped off, so that the ship would not have to carry its useless weight. Then, the next stage would begin to burn.

Finally, with all three of the Saturn 5 stages burnt out and shed along the way, the Apollo moonship would be on its own, heading for the moon. The Apollo would be made up of three sections: the Command Module (where the three astronauts would ride), the Service Module (the equipment and rocket unit behind the Command Module), and the Lunar Module (the small spacecraft in which two men would ferry to and from the moon's surface).

Having made the decision of how to get to the moon, the Apollo Project planners were then faced with the enormous task of mobilizing the men and resources, designing and building the machines, and perfecting the techniques for the mission.

CHAPTER 4

Robot
Pathfinders

Little was known about space travel in 1961. No American astronaut had even orbited the earth yet. No American spacecraft had journeyed to the moon. No one, neither the scientists nor the engineers, could be sure that the moon was a safe place for a landing.

Yet once the Apollo decision was made, we reached out in an incredibly short span of time to touch the moon. These first missions were carried out by robot spacecraft. They photographed the moon's surface, picked at its soil, and analyzed its rocks. They orbited around the moon many times, testing its gravitational forces and mapping good landing spots.

It was necessary to see what the moon was like, whether or

not it was safe to land men there and, if so, where would be the best landing sites. To answer these questions, the United States mounted three unmanned lunar exploration projects in the 1960's —Ranger, Surveyor, and Lunar Orbiter.

These robot scouting parties for Apollo were controlled from a quiet research center nestled against the San Gabriel Mountains on the outskirts of Pasadena, California. This is the Jet Propulsion Laboratory (JPL). One of the nation's oldest space research centers, it built the first American spacecraft, Explorer 1, and designed vehicles to pass by Venus and Mars as well as to go to the moon.

Exploring the moon with unmanned spacecraft turned out to be no easy task. The United States recorded twelve moonshot failures before finally succeeding with Ranger 7 in 1964. The Soviet Union was only slightly more successful. One of its vehicles, called Luna 2, smashed almost dead center into the front side of the moon on September 12, 1959, to become the first man-made object to touch another world. Three weeks later, Luna 3 flew around the back of the moon, returning the first photographs of the side always hidden from earth viewers. Though rather blurred and grainy, the pictures showed that the moon's far side, like its front, was pitted with craters. But after these successful missions, several Soviet moonflights met with failure in the years between 1959 and 1966.

RANGER

The Ranger Project, the first step in America's lunar exploration, was actually started before Apollo. In 1959, NASA officials asked JPL to design a spacecraft that could take close-up pictures of the moon's surface. The craft they had in mind would help scientists to learn about moonflight and would also give them a clear view of lunar features never before seen by man.

The JPL engineers came up with a ship that weighed about 800 pounds and, in flight, looked like a giant dragonfly. Ranger's wings were its two solar panels, extending 15 feet from tip to tip. These were designed to absorb the sun's energy and change it to electricity to run the spacecraft's instruments. The body of the spacecraft was ten feet long with an instrument section in the front and with a narrow tail where television cameras were mounted. With the new Atlas-Agena rocket as the launcher, the Ranger would first go into an earth orbit and then, with the refiring of the Agena, shoot out toward the moon, sending television pictures back to earth during the last 20 minutes of flight, before crashing into the lunar face.

The first two Rangers, launched in 1961, never got out of earth orbit. The Agena failed to restart. Three more Rangers, more advanced models than the first two, were launched in 1962. But they, too, were failures. An aiming error of the Atlas booster caused Ranger 3 to miss the moon by about 23,000 miles. Ranger 4's control system short-circuited, sending the spacecraft crashing into the far side of the moon. Ranger 5's power system went dead before it reached the moon. Ranger 6 followed a perfect course to the moon's Sea of Tranquility, but then it plunged toward the surface with its television cameras dead. There were no pictures.

Finally, Ranger 7 was launched on July 28, 1964. It worked. The 807-pound package of six television cameras beamed 4,300 pictures back to earth before hitting the Sea of Clouds. They showed craters as small as 3 feet in diameter and some rocks no more than 10 inches wide—features that no earth-based telescope could have picked out.

In 1965, Rangers 8 and 9 repeated Ranger 7's success, sending back 12,951 high-quality pictures of the moon. Ranger 8 photographed the Sea of Tranquility and Ranger 9 focused on the highlands area near the Sea of Clouds.

The Ranger pictures were the first evidence that many areas

of the moon were smooth enough for manned landings. Geologists were surprised, in fact, to find so few boulders and loose rocks on the lunar surface. Still, no one could be sure that the surface was firm enough to support a 15-ton landing craft. The pictures settled few of the scientific arguments over the nature of the moon's surface. People still did not know whether it was blanketed with dust, whether it was porous and crumbly, or whether its craters had been caused by volcanoes or by meteors.

SURVEYOR

It was left to a spidery, three-legged spacecraft called Surveyor to furnish a more spectacular and exact report on lunar conditions. The Surveyor was designed to land softly on the moon, photograph its immediate surroundings, test the "bearing strength," or firmness, of the lunar surface, and even run a chemical test of the soil.

Surveyor was the most complex piece of space machinery of its day. Into its triangular aluminum frame were packed fuel tanks, small guidance rockets, various sensing devices, and the guidance equipment on which the soft landing depended—radar, computer, autopilot, and the braking rocket. Its total weight at lift-off was at least 2,200 pounds. After finding its way across 240,000 miles of space, Surveyor was expected, on command from the ground, to point its braking rocket toward the moon at a slant. At about 200 miles above the surface, the on-board radar had to switch on and, at 60 miles, the radar had to order the braking rocket to fire. This blast was to slow Surveyor from a speed of 6,000 miles an hour to 250 miles an hour. Another radar, similar to one astronauts would later use for their lunar descent, would begin bouncing signals off the moon to help Surveyor feel its way to the surface. It was up to three smaller rocket engines to apply more braking thrust until the spacecraft was 14 feet off the lunar ground. Then, with all engines shut off, the craft would fall the rest of the way.

While Surveyor was still untried and unproven, the Soviet Union was also trying to land on the moon. Its first five soft-landing efforts were failures. Finally, on January 31, 1966, a Soviet spacecraft named Luna 9 reached the moon's surface in working order.

From Russian accounts, it appeared that Luna 9 was fairly crude compared to Surveyor. Just before it crashed on the moon, it tossed out a 220-pound sphere that was about twice the diameter of a basketball. As the sphere bounced onto the moon, its outer case dropped away like flower petals, exposing a single television camera. The spacecraft returned 27 pictures of rocks and soil before its batteries died.

About two months later, on April 3, Luna 10 became the first vehicle ever to go into orbit around the moon. The 3,500-pound spacecraft carried instruments to measure the moon's radiation and magnetism, if any, and to study the material of the moon's crust. But it apparently had no camera.

A study of Luna 10's data led to the first strong evidence that the moon, like earth, was once molten, and that its lighter rocks had risen to form a crust.

With high hopes, American space officials gathered at Cape Kennedy in May for the launching of the first Surveyor. On June 2, after a flight of more than 63 hours, Surveyor 1 landed softly on the Ocean of Storms near the crater Flamsteed. Its rotating television camera went into action and transmitted 11,150 black and white pictures before the long lunar night set in.

At a news conference in Washington after Surveyor's picture-taking days were over, Leonard Jaffe, JPL's project scientist, said: "The moon surface looks like a soil, not very hard, with rocks and clods on it and in it." Jaffe also said that the pictures showed clumps of material like wet soil. Such clumping was expected because small particles tend to stick together in a deep vacuum like that on the moon. Other scientists said they identified some pock-marked rock that looked like lava in which bubbles of gas have burst during cooling.

Four of the remaining six Surveyors were equally successful. They showed once and for all that the moon was a safe place for manned landings.

Surveyor 2 was launched in September, four months after the initial success and a month behind another Soviet moon-orbiting craft, Luna 11. This Surveyor was aimed at the Central Bay (Sinus Medii), but a failure of one of its maneuvering rockets sent it into a wild tumbling flight to crash landing.

Then, on April 3, 1967, Surveyor 3 landed gently on the Ocean of Storms and did more than take pictures. It stretched out a robot arm and dug a hole in the surface of the moon with a sharp metal claw. With slow, sometimes jerky movements, the mechanical arm extended itself nearly 5 feet on commands radioed from the control room on the earth. The experiment showed that lunar soil was fine-grained stuff that stuck together like damp clods.

Surveyor 4 was a failure. Signals stopped suddenly within 7 miles of the moon's Central Bay. Surveyor 5 landed successfully on the moon. Its measurements showed that the lunar rocks seemed to be like basalt, a material that forms the bedrock of the Palisades of the Hudson River, the Hawaiian Islands, and Iceland.

This was by far the most interesting of Surveyor's findings. It made scientists all the more eager to get their hands on the samples of lunar soil that the Apollo astronauts would bring back. It even made a few scientists pause and wonder if perhaps the scientist George Darwin had not been right when he suggested that the moon was a chunk of our planet that spun off from the Pacific basin when the earth was young.

Surveyor 6, which landed in the Central Bay on November 9 sent back more pictures and soil analysis. The last of the Surveyors, Surveyor 7, was aimed at the rugged highland region near Tycho, the relatively new and brightly rayed crater at the south of the moon's face. After Surveyor 7 landed on January 9, 1968, its instruments showed that there was less iron there than in the Sea of Tranquility, but otherwise the moonrock seemed to be about the same.

Thus, the Surveyors, after a slow start, proved to be excellent pathfinders for Apollo. Benjamin Milwitsky, the Surveyor program manager at NASA headquarters, said the awkward-looking vehicles "established that the moon is entirely suitable for Apollo landings. We've established that a spacecraft on the moon will not sink in deeply, that an astronaut will not need snowshoes to stay on top."

LUNAR ORBITER

At about the same time, another series of unmanned spacecraft—the Lunar Orbiters—were taking a different sort of look at the moon. From an orbit about 26 to 28 miles above the surface, they focused their cameras on a 3,000-mile strip along the lunar equator on the side visible to earth. This was the zone where astronauts would land, and Apollo planners wanted it completely mapped. All of the five Lunar Orbiters were successful in doing their mapping.

Compared to Surveyor, Lunar Orbiter was a fairly simple spacecraft. In flight, it looked a little like a four-leaf clover. The center section was the body, housing the camera, radio, and television equipment, and the rocket that fired the craft into lunar orbit. Sticking out from the body were two antennas and four solar panels—the four clover leaves. The 850-pound craft was launched by the Atlas-Agena rocket.

Lunar Orbiter 1 landed on August 10, 1966, and focused on nine promising Apollo landing sites to the south of the equator.

When Lunar Orbiter 2 began circling the moon on November 15, 1966, it made a similar survey of sites to the north of the equator. On February 8, 1967, the third Orbiter began re-examining the most promising Apollo sites, taking overlapping pictures that would bring out the shape of the surface.

Since the first three Orbiters were so successful, giving Apollo planners all they needed in the way of landing-site pictures, the last two flights were devoted to targets of great scientific interest. Both Orbiter 4 and Orbiter 5 circled the moon from its north pole to its south pole, rather than at its equator. In this way, they were able to photograph 99 per cent of the surface as it rotated under them. Orbiter 4 reached the moon in May of 1967; Orbiter 5 completed the series in August of that year.

One of the project's most important discoveries came from the way the Lunar Orbiters moved in their orbits. They had a curious way of dipping and wiggling when their orbits took them closest to the moon's surface. They were occasionally drawn three to six miles nearer the surface than they should have been. In 1968, after months of analysis, two JPL mathematicians—Paul M. Muller and William L. Sjogren—offered a reason when they noticed that the dips had happened during passes over circular crater-like seas—the Seas of Rains, Serenity, Crises, Nectar, and Moisture.

They reported that this dipping could be explained if there were large, dense concentrations of mass lying beneath these seas. They called the concentrations "mascons." According to one theory, the mascons could be the remains of meteors that had collided with the moon, melted from the heat of collision, cooled, and then settled into the moon's surface.

By the end of 1967, NASA had narrowed to five the number of promising sites for the first astronaut landing. Two were in the Sea of Tranquility, one on the eastern side, one in the Central Bay, and two more on the western side of the Ocean of Storms. As the robot pathfinders had discovered, these were safe, firm, and fairly smooth areas.

CHAPTER 5

Human
Pathfinders

Beyond our sheltering atmosphere lie the great stretches of space. Space is airless and seems to be completely empty. But it is not exactly true that it is empty because it is flooded with invisible radiation.

Men in space must take their own air with them in order to breathe. They must be protected from extreme heat when the sun is shining on their ship and from extreme cold when the ship lies in the shadow of the earth or moon. They must learn to live in "free fall," the weightless condition in an orbiting ship where there is no feeling of up or down. Only when the ship's rocket blasts does there seem to be any up or down—then the force of the blast makes the back end of the ship seem like a floor. The rest of the time, the astronauts drift in their cabin like goldfish in a bowl.

Before the first men went into space, some scientists wondered if people could stand such strange conditions. Some thought that the astronauts might be very confused by the silence and loneliness and the floating, weightless condition in an orbiting spaceship. Others thought the human bones and heart might be damaged if astronauts were in free fall for a long time. The heart might be weakened by having too little work to do and might not be able to stand the strain of coming back to earth. There were also those who feared that the bones would begin to lose calcium, as happens when a person lies in bed for weeks. And—who could tell?—there might be other types of damage that no one would expect.

However, a larger number of scientists felt that conditions in a spaceship would not seriously harm astronauts—at least in short flights.

But what about the difficulty of getting men into space? Could engineers check on all the things that could go wrong and build spacecraft safe enough for human passengers? No one could be sure in 1961. Every so often a rocket would blow up in flames on the launching pad. Spacecraft got into orbit and then, when some electrical part failed, went dead. There was the question of building a ship light enough to get into space but strong enough to stand radiation, collisions with meteorites the size of sand grains, and the heat and vibrations of the return to earth.

The only way to be sure that Americans could build and fly space vehicles designed to carry human beings was to do it. This was the main purpose of the two manned flight projects that went before Apollo—Mercury and Gemini.

MERCURY

"We are behind," President Kennedy said after the Soviet

Union's Yuri Gagarin orbited the earth in April, 1961, in Vostok 1, "and it will be some time before we catch up."

It took about ten months.

On May 5, 1961, Alan B. Shepard, Jr., became the first American to venture into space—but it was far short of an orbital flight. He rode a Mercury spacecraft 302 miles down range from the Florida launching pad. During his fifteen minutes in space, he reached a height of 115 miles above the ground. Both the astronaut and the capsule were recovered in the ocean, proving that both could stand a short space flight. Shepard was in a weightless state only about four minutes. "The only complaint I have," said Shepard, "was the flight was not long enough."

Less than three months later, on July 21, 1961, Virgil I. "Gus" Grissom piloted another Mercury capsule along the same suborbital path. When Grissom splashed down, the explosive mechanism on the escape hatch went off accidentally, blowing the hatch open. Grissom swam free and was rescued by a waiting helicopter, but the capsule sank.

Both Shepard and Grissom had been launched by Redstone rockets, which were not powerful enough to boost them into orbit. The more powerful Atlas booster was still undergoing test firings with Mercury capsules, holding chimpanzees and robots. Until the Atlas was tested and ready, no Americans could become true orbiting spacemen.

The Soviet Union put its second manned spaceship into orbit two weeks after Grissom's flight. Gherman S. Titov, a 26-year-old Air Force major, circled the earth 17 times at altitudes from 110 to 160 miles and returned safely, touching down on land inside the Soviet Union. Titov's flight raised some doubts about man's ability to stand spaceflight. Titov wrote later: "For the life of me, I could not determine where I was. I felt suddenly as though I were turning a somersault and then flying with my legs up. I was completely confused, unable to define where was earth or the stars . . . My sense of orientation vanished abruptly and completely."

John H. Glenn, Jr., was the first American astronaut to make an orbital flight. After weeks of delay, he finally walked out to the launching pad before dawn on February 20, 1962. Thousands watched the Atlas and Mercury from the Canaveral beaches. Millions more throughout the country sat before television sets. At 9:17 A.M. the Atlas gave a thunderous roar and slowly rose.

Unlike Titov, Glenn found that the feeling of weightlessness was very pleasant. He never felt at all uncomfortable. He had no difficulty taking food from squeeze tubes. And he said that the view was "tremendous."

The flight had some tense moments. During the first three orbits, trouble developed with the small rockets that automatically controlled the tilt of the capsule. Glenn took over manual control of the rockets. Also, in the control room, a warning light showed that the capsule's plastic-glass heat shield had become unlatched. If the shield fell off, Glenn would be incinerated when the capsule plunged back into the earth's atmosphere.

A decision was made not to drop off the retro-rockets after they were fired. The hope was that the straps attached to the retro-pack, the unit holding the retro-rockets, which passed over the heat shield, might hold the shield in place. When the Mercury—Glenn called it Friendship 7—re-entered the atmosphere, the retro-pack flew off in "big, flaming chunks." Watching them sail past the capsule window, Glenn felt that the heat shield might be coming apart. Still, he stayed calm. "Boy, that was a real fireball," he reported to Mercury control. But the shield stayed in place, and Glenn's capsule hit the water near the recovery ship. After three orbits of earth, Glenn reported, "My condition is excellent."

What was this Mercury capsule like that these astronauts had flown so successfully? The main body of Mercury was shaped like a bell. It was 9 feet 7 inches long from the base of the blunt heat shield to the tip of the barrel-shaped nose. It was 6 feet 2 inches wide at its widest point, the blunt end, and weighed about 3,000 pounds. The nose contained radio antennas and control systems as well as the parachutes for landing. Mounted on the blunt end were the three retro-rockets needed to brake the spacecraft for the descent to earth. To save weight, the engineers decided that the cabin atmosphere should be pure oxygen at about one-third the pressure at sea level instead of a mixture of nitrogen and oxygen, which is more like normal atmosphere.

After Glenn's flight, three more astronauts took their turns orbiting in the Mercury. On May 24, 1962, M. Scott Carpenter became the second American to circle the earth. His three-orbit trip ended in suspense. As a result of a re-entry error, Carpenter's capsule overshot its landing point by 250 miles and, for a time, was out of radio contact with the recovery ship. But soon, the astronaut was found safe in his capsule. The mission was a success.

On October 3, 1962, Walter M. Schirra, Jr., took the next ride in Mercury. It lasted nine hours as he circled the earth six times in the most flawless mission to date.

The project was brought to a successful conclusion in May, 1963, with the 22-orbit, 34-hour flight of L. Gordon Cooper, who, at 36, was the youngest of the original seven astronauts. Toward the end of Cooper's flight, a failure in the equipment forced the astronaut to take over the controls himself. He manually guided the craft all the way down to a bulls-eye splashdown. "Right on the old gazoo," Cooper radioed.

Cooper's was the last of the Mercury flights. After six manned voyages, lasting a total of 51 hours and 40 minutes, Mercury had served its purpose. Men had gone into space and survived. Besides, they seemed able to work and think while in orbit and there had been no bad effects.

The Mercury Project had scarcely ended before the Soviet Union launched yet another Vostok, its fifth. After the Gagarin and

Titov missions in 1961, the Russians had outdistanced Mercury with a four-day manned flight in August, 1962. Andrian Nikolayev rode Vostok 3 for 64 orbits. While Nikolayev was aloft, Pavel Popovich was launched in Vostok 4 for a three-day, 48-orbit flight. The launching was timed and aimed so that Vostok 4 came within 3.1 miles of Vostok 3. For the fifth Vostok mission, nearly a year later in June, 1963, Valery Bykovsky orbited the earth 81 times and was joined in space by the first woman cosmonaut, Valentina Tereshkova, in Vostok 6. Though they did not accomplish a rendezvous, the two cosmonauts landed safely two and a half hours and 50 miles apart.

GEMINI

Gemini was a two-man spacecraft in which astronauts showed that they could steer through many of the maneuvers necessary for a flight to the moon. The Gemini spacecraft was larger and more maneuverable than the Mercury. The crew capsule was shaped a little like a bell and it had a blunt end shielded against fiery re-entry. It was 11 feet high and $7\frac{1}{2}$ feet wide at the base. The weight of the capsule and its equipment unit was more than 7,000 pounds. The capsule contained radar for rendezvous maneuvers and a computer the size of a hatbox to solve in-flight problems.

The first two Gemini flights were unmanned tests of both the rocket, the more powerful Titan 2 military missile, and the spacecraft. No attempt was made to return and recover Gemini 1, launched into orbit on April 8, 1964. The second unmanned flight, in January, 1965, demonstrated successfully the craft's ability to withstand the heat and stress of re-entry.

Meanwhile, the Russians orbited the world's first multi-man spaceflight—three men in Voskhod 1, which circled the earth 16 times in October, 1964. And, on March 18, 1965, before Gemini 3 could be launched, the Russians sent up Voskhod 2 for a 17-orbit flight. It had two men aboard and one of them, Alexei Leonov, became the first human being to step outside an orbiting vehicle for a floating "walk" in space.

Less than a week later, on March 23, Grissom and John W. Young, a member of the second "class" of astronauts, selected in 1962, were launched in Gemini 3. Though it was a short flight —3 orbits—the two men had time to show that Gemini could be steered up and down, right and left, backward and forward, and could even change orbits. A set of sixteen thruster rockets ringing the vehicle made this possible.

On June 3, Gemini 4 was launched on a 4-day, 62-orbit flight during which Edward H. White became the first American to "walk" in space. White enjoyed his space walk so much that it took a little coaxing by his commander, James A. McDivitt, to get him back inside the capsule. For 20 minutes, he chatted, joked, and snapped pictures as he darted about in raw space, using a gas-firing jet gun to move from place to place. The bursts from the gun caused a recoil that pushed him in the opposite direction. Of course, that is the same thing that makes a rocket work. The recoil from the rocket blast is what pushes the ship forward. The same kind of force is at work when you let go of a rubber balloon full of air, with an untied neck. It is the recoil from the air squirting out through the neck of the balloon that makes it dart crazily through the air.

Next came Gemini 5. Cooper, the Mercury astronaut, and Charles P. Conrad, Jr., a rookie, began their planned 8-day mission on August 21, 1965.

A chemical "fuel cell" was used in Gemini 5 instead of an electric battery. The fuel cell, which used chemical reactions to generate electricity, was lighter than the batteries used in earlier flights. A fuel-cell system was already being planned for Apollo.

Early in the first day of Gemini 5's flight, the fuel cell began to fail. The astronauts flew a perfect mission anyway. The flight surgeon reported later that they had come through their 8-day trip in perfect health.

In December, 1965, Gemini 6 and Gemini 7 were launched and met each other in orbit. On board Gemini 6 were astronauts Schirra and Thomas P. Stafford. Gemini 7 was manned by Frank Borman and James A. Lovell, Jr. The two crafts came within a foot of each other and, for several hours, circled the earth in formation. "A piece of cake," Schirra said afterward, describing the beautiful rendezvous maneuvers.

Even a close shave on March 16, 1966, did not stop the Gemini team. On that date Gemini 8 was launched and made the first docking with another orbiting vehicle, a 27-foot-long unmanned Agena. It was "like parking a car," Neil A. Armstrong, the command pilot, said.

Then trouble struck. Gemini 8 began bucking and spinning wildly because of a misfiring thruster rocket. Armstrong and David R. Scott, the other crew member, were forced to make an emergency splashdown in the Pacific before the end of their first day in space.

In the last four Gemini flights, astronauts practiced over and over the techniques of rendezvous and docking and gained more experience operating outside their orbiting craft.

Gemini 9 was the three-day mission in which Stafford and Eugene A. Cernan used three different approaches to rendezvous with a target. No docking was tried because the protective clamshell shroud failed to break free of the target's docking collar. With jaws wide open, it looked to Stafford like "an angry alligator." Cernan performed a long space walk before the flight ended on June 6.

Young and Michael Collins took a 3-day trip in Gemini 10, beginning July 18. They achieved the first double rendezvous, first with their Agena and then with the still-orbiting Agena left over from the Gemini 8 mission. They docked with their own Agena.

On September 12, Gemini 11 was launched. During its 3-day flight, Conrad and Richard F. Gordon, Jr., linked up with an Agena and then fired the Agena's main engine to propel themselves 850 miles out from earth, the farthest man had ventured at the time.

For the last Gemini flight (Gemini 12), Lovell and Edwin E. Aldrin, Jr., raced into orbit on November 11 and, despite a balky radar unit, steered their craft to a successful rendezvous and docking with an Agena. They splashed down 4 days later, after many rendezvous maneuvers and Aldrin's $5\frac{1}{2}$ hours of space walking.

In the ten manned Gemini flights, American astronauts spent a total of 969 hours and 56 minutes in space. The experience in rendezvous and docking was important to Apollo planning, because the landing craft and the Apollo would have to rendezvous and dock in lunar orbit before the return to earth. The long Gemini flights also proved that man could survive in space for the 7 or 8 days it should take for a round trip to the moon. The Gemini space walks gave astronauts a feeling of what it would be like to work in the low-gravity conditions that exist on the moon and were good practice for emergency operations if there were any trouble docking in lunar orbit.

CHAPTER 6

The Men Who Were Lost

From November, 1963, through the end of 1965, there were ten unmanned launchings in which various Apollo systems were tested. In the first full-scale unmanned test, on February 26, 1966, the spacecraft, including the Command Module and the Service Module, was fired 5,500 miles down the Atlantic Missile Range by a Saturn 1-B, forerunner of the Saturn 5. The rocket engine needed for lunar-orbiting maneuvers was fired and refired but did not blast at full power. Even so, Apollo officials rated the flight a "successful first step."

Two more tests were run in the summer of 1966. On July 5, a dummy payload was put into earth orbit to test the rocket stage that would boost men out of near-earth orbit toward the moon.

This was the engine S-4B that would be the third stage of the Saturn 5. The test was successful. Equally successful was a second launching on August 25, when an unmanned Apollo rose from Cape Kennedy on an 18,000-mile flight that ended in a Pacific Ocean splashdown. The spacecraft's engine fired perfectly and the heat shield withstood the temperature and pressure of a re-entry from space into the air.

The spacecraft for the first manned Apollo mission was shipped to Cape Kennedy in the summer of 1966. Then, came many months of testing and repairing troubles in the spacecraft. These difficulties went on for about a half a year. On January 27, 1967, three astronauts entered the Apollo capsule for ground tests. In these tests, the Apollo would never leave the ground and the rocket engines of the Saturn 1-B would not even be fired. The astronauts who were carrying out these tests were Roger B. Chaffee, a 31-year-old lieutenant commander in the Navy, Edward H. White, a 36-year-old lieutenant colonel in the Air Force, and Gus Grissom, also an Air Force lieutenant colonel and a veteran of two spaceflights—the second Mercury and the first Gemini.

On that Friday afternoon, the three fully suited astronauts lay strapped in the couches of Apollo 1—Grissom on the left, White in the middle, and Chaffee on the right. The spacecraft was perched on top of the Saturn 1-B, the two of them standing a total of 224 feet tall. Around it was the protective steel latticework of the 310-foot-high service tower, which provided platforms for workmen. Test conductors kept instrument watch on Apollo 1 from the "white room," the enclosed uppermost platform nearest the spacecraft, and from a blockhouse about 1,000 feet away.

Apart from the rocket's not being loaded with fuel, it was a realistic rehearsal of how the final countdown was to go. It was not considered a "hazardous" test because of the unloaded rocket. So everyone was somewhat relaxed and there were no emergency crews of firemen and doctors on hand.

With the astronauts inside the spacecraft, the hatch had been closed and sealed and the cabin pumped full of pure oxygen to a pressure of 16.7 pounds a square inch, 2 pounds higher than normal sea-level atmosphere. This was the way Apollo was to be pressurized while awaiting lift-off. Then there had come many delays as different things went wrong with various pieces of electrical equipment.

By 6:30 P.M., the countdown was finally moving along. Then, there came a sudden and terrible interruption. An electrical spark or short circuit inside the oxygen-rich cabin flooded the cabin with fire. The entire inside of the cabin filled with flames and smoke. There was no way to open the hatch quickly, either from the inside or from the outside. The three astronauts had soon died.

Slowly, after the shock of the launch-pad tragedy, the Apollo planners and engineers began to redesign the system. New safeguards (such as a quick-opening hatch) were built into the Apollo.

Plans were laid for a new flight, with Schirra, Walter Cunningham, and Donn Eisele as the crew. As the people of Apollo picked up the pieces, the memory of Grissom, White, and Chaffee was real and haunting. But what the Apollo people remembered more and more was not the astronauts' deaths but something Grissom had said. "If we die," he once had said, "we want people to accept it. We are in a risky business, and we hope that if anything happens to us it will not delay the program. The conquest of space is worth the risk of life."

THE RUSSIANS ALSO MEET WITH TRAGEDY

Until 1967, Russian cosmonauts had gone into space in two classes of spacecraft, the Vostoks and Voskhods. There were six manned missions in a Vostok (two each in 1961, 1962, and 1963) and two flights in a Voskhod (one each in 1964 and 1965). But such was the secrecy of the Soviet program that not until a few years later did Westerners get a fairly clear picture of these vehicles and their launching rockets.

The one-man Vostok was large and spherical and weighed roughly 10,400 pounds, about $3\frac{1}{2}$ times as much as the Mercury. Vostok was roomier than Mercury. Its diameter was about 8 feet. There were two compartments, one for the pilot and one for the equipment. Those who had been inside a Vostok cockpit described it as much simpler than Mercury's, apparently containing fewer dials, gauges, and switches. One major difference was the cabin atmosphere. Instead of the low-pressure pure oxygen that American astronauts breathed, the Vostok cabin was pumped full of mixed gases (24 per cent oxygen and the rest primarily nitrogen) to a pressure almost like that at sea level. In other words, it was almost identical to the air we ordinarily breathe. The thicker walls of Vostok made it possible to maintain such a pressure, which might have ruptured the thin Mercury walls. Like the American craft, Vostok was equipped with braking rockets and parachutes for the return to earth. But it was designed so that when it got near the ground, the hatch opened automatically and, moments later, the pilot in his seat was explosively ejected. He came down to earth by parachute as the capsule floated down a separate chute.

The Russians shifted from the Vostok series to the Voskhod flights after they developed more powerful rockets. Western space experts think that the Voskhod was nothing but an improved Vostok. The same 8-foot sphere was rearranged so that three astronauts could sit side by side. The first manned Voskhod, sent aloft in October, 1964, weighed 11,731 pounds and carried a crew of three.

The second Voskhod, launched 5 months later, was heavier, weighing 12,529 pounds. It was heavier, although it carried two cosmonauts instead of three, because it included a submarine-like airlock. It was through this chamber that Alexei A. Leonov crawled to begin man's first "walk" in raw space. (This happened before the Gemini space walks.) When it came time for re-entry from orbit, Voskhod 2's automatic system failed to work properly. The cosmonauts had to wait another orbit and then steer the ship down to earth. Instead of landing in the open country of the Ukraine, where recovery teams were waiting, they came down far to the north in a snowbound forest. It took hours for the ship to be found and about a day for ground parties to break through the isolated woods to reach the crew and bring them out on skis.

Then came the launch of an advanced Soviet spacecraft, the Soyuz, on April 23, 1967, and in that mission, death came to a Soviet cosmonaut. His name was Vladimir M. Komarov and he had already been on a space mission in Voskhod 1.

The Soyuz had a disastrous re-entry from space. According to Soviet reports, Komarov died when the Soyuz plunged through the atmosphere and, with the parachute lines hopelessly tangled, crashed into the ground.

Many Russians broke into tears when the news was broadcast. The tragedy was a great shock to the Russian people, who had looked to the flight to help them regain their space leadership. There had been talk of a whole series of Soyuz missions throughout the summer. But now that this accident had happened, the Soyuz spacecraft would have to be studied and improved.

The three American astronauts and the one Russian cosmonaut who died inside their spaceships were brave men. Their calm and strength in carrying out dangerous missions were among the good qualities that they were chosen for. They died because it was important to them that man be able to explore the great universe around him—important enough so that they were ready to risk their lives for it.

CHAPTER 7

The Saturn-Apollo

The Apollo spaceship, mounted on top of the Saturn 5 booster, is called the "Saturn-Apollo." There are many parts to the Saturn-Apollo, and, to understand the things that happened in the first moon trip, it is useful to know about these parts and how they work.

Everything about the Saturn 5 is big. When topped with the Apollo spacecraft, the three-stage rocket stands 363 feet tall, six stories higher than the Statue of Liberty. Its first, or booster stage, is the biggest aluminum cylinder ever machined. Its valves are as big as barrels, its fuel pumps are bigger than refrigerators, its fuel lines are big enough for a man to crawl through, and its engines are the size of trucks.

THE LAUNCH VEHICLE

Five F-1 engines   **Interstage unit**   **Five J-2 engines**

Five F-1 engines: Launch vehicle with 7.5 million pounds of thrust. **Interstage unit:** Connects first two stages and contains equipment for both. **Five J-2 engines:** Take rocket to altitude for earth orbit with more than a million pounds of thrust. **Single J-2 engine:** Puts vehicle into orbit with 200,000 pounds of thrust.

There are four main sections to the Saturn 5. The first-stage rocket is the biggest of these sections. As the tail-end section of the Saturn-Apollo, it is the first rocket to blast. Therefore, its blast must be powerful enough to lift the entire Saturn-Apollo up from the launch pad and hurl it toward outer space. It does not do this great task by using any special fuel mixture. In fact, it uses a mixture that is a fairly old-fashioned rocket fuel: liquid oxygen and kerosene.

By itself, the stage is bigger than any single previous rocket —138 feet tall and 33 feet in diameter. Its weight is more than three-quarters the weight of the entire Saturn-Apollo.

Clustered at the base of the stage are five engines, each 18 feet tall, that burn all their fuel in $2\frac{1}{2}$ minutes to force a fiery exhaust out their five bell-shaped nozzles. In these $2\frac{1}{2}$ minutes, the five engines use as much fuel as three million automobiles would use if they ran for $2\frac{1}{2}$ minutes each. Each engine blasts with 1.5 million pounds of thrust, making the total rocket thrust of the stage 7.5 million pounds.* With this power, it boosts the

* The thrusting force of a rocket is measured in pounds. A one-pound force is the force that would barely lift a one-pound weight off the ground. A one-million-pound thrust would barely lift a one-million-pound weight off the ground. A rocket engine must have enough thrust to lift a spaceship off the ground *and* to speed it upward.

APOLLO SPACECRAFT

Single J-2 engine

Lunar module

Service module

Command module

Launch escape system

Lunar module: On lunar flight, will take two astronauts to the surface of the moon. **Service module:** Contains support systems for command module and power to maneuver it. **Command module:** "Home" for the three astronauts on their way to the moon and back. **Launch escape system:** Carries command module free of rocket in case of accident.

Saturn-Apollo 38 miles through the air to a speed of almost 6,100 miles an hour. Then, the burnt-out first stage disconnects and drops away.

Perched on the shoulders of the booster is the second stage, the most powerful hydrogen-fueled rocket ever built. It is 81 feet 7 inches high and 33 feet in diameter, and has five rocket engines. Its tanks hold 267,700 gallons of super-cold liquid hydrogen and 87,000 gallons of liquid oxygen, or "Lox." Unlike air-breathing jet engines, rocket engines carry their own oxygen** supplies. Otherwise, out in airless space, they could not fire at all.

The five engines of the second stage were designed to develop up to 225,000 pounds of thrust each, or 1,125,000 pounds for the entire stage. They burn for about 6 minutes, pushing the Saturn-Apollo to an altitude of about 115 miles and a speed of 15,300 miles an hour—just short of orbit. Then, they too burn out and drop away.

The third and uppermost stage of the Saturn 5 blasts the fast-moving ship into orbit. The third stage is 58 feet 7 inches high and 21 feet 8 inches in diameter, and carries 63,000 gallons of liquid hydrogen and 20,000 gallons of liquid oxygen.

** Some rockets use other chemicals in place of oxygen.

The stage's single engine fires when the vehicle is approaching orbit. By firing more than 2 minutes, boosting the ship's speed to 17,400 miles an hour, the third-stage rocket blasts the ship into orbit. On a voyage to the moon, the engine burns again for about 5 minutes to boost the astronauts out of their low earth orbit and on the way to the moon.

Finally, there is a 3-foot-high section on top of the Saturn 5 that is the rocket's electronic brain. Signals from this computer send instructions to the different stages, to ignite and shut down the engines and to check on their operation.

Just to get the many parts of the Saturn 5 to Cape Kennedy was a hard task. The first stage went by special barge from the Mississippi Test Facility on the Gulf of Mexico. The second stage was shipped by barge from California through the Panama Canal. The third stage and other smaller parts were sent to the Cape in an oversized transport plane called the "Super Guppy." They were all put together—"mated," as the engineers called it—in a 525-foot-tall building near the launching pad.

Inside this building, the Saturn 5's took shape, stage by stage. Once a Saturn 5 rocket was put together, it had to be moved out to the launch pad. A special, strong roadway had to be built, packed with river rocks. Along this road, a huge tractor-like vehicle as big as a baseball diamond carried the Saturns to their launch pads. The $3\frac{1}{2}$-mile journey to the launch pad was nearly 8 hours long.

On November 9, 1967, the Saturn 5 was used to boost an unmanned model of Apollo into space. This test was the Apollo 4 mission. When the launch countdown reached zero, the five engines of the first stage fired, sending gushes of orange flame and smoke over the launching pad. A million gallons of water rushed into the concrete "flame bucket" underneath to prevent serious damage to the pad. As soon as instruments showed that all five engines were firing evenly, the steel "hold arms" on the nearby mobile tower loosened their grip on the spaceship. At 7 A.M., on schedule, the

36-story spaceship began to rise from its pad in a mushroom of smoke.

Not until the rocket cleared the launch tower, about 10 seconds after lift-off, did the shock wave reach the press site 16,000 feet away. It traveled through the ground and the air. The roar of Saturn 5 shook the small wooden grandstand, rattled its iron roof, and pushed in the plate glass window on a CBS mobile studio. Reporters in the open could feel the pressure of the shock wave beating at their faces and chests. Inside the launch control center, everything was covered with plaster dust that had shaken loose from the ceiling.

Each of the Saturn's three stages fired on schedule. When the third stage stopped burning, 11 minutes after lift-off, the unmanned Apollo spacecraft that had been on top of the rocket was orbiting earth. Unlike the other stages, the third one remained attached to the spacecraft. Later, it refired to drive the spacecraft 11,286 miles out from earth.

The rocket's third stage and a dummy lunar module, taken along to make it a realistic test of the full Saturn-Apollo, were then dropped away. On a signal from ground controllers, the Apollo's main rocket fired to ram the command module back down through the air at a speed of about 24,500 miles an hour, the speed it would travel on a return from the moon. This gave the command module's heat shield its first test at such re-entry speeds and temperatures. After a mission of 8 hours and 40 minutes, the command module splashed down in the Pacific northwest of Hawaii.

The second flight of the Saturn 5 was less successful. On April 4, 1968, another Saturn 5 was launched in a test of the rocket and of the Apollo spacecraft—the Apollo 6 mission. But two of the second stage engines burned out too soon and the third stage engine failed to reignite in orbit.

For a time, it appeared that NASA would have to conduct a third unmanned Saturn 5 launching before the mighty rocket could be "man-rated"—cleared for launching men. But engineers found out that the engine troubles were caused by vibrations that could easily be prevented.

The Saturn 5, the most powerful rocket in the world, was ready to launch astronauts into space.

THE LANDING BUG

The lunar module of the Apollo is a strange, awkward-looking craft. It has an oddly shaped body mounted on four spindly, jointed legs. It looks like a live creature, and that is why people have called it the "spider," the "moonbug," or the "landing bug." Compared with the huge, streamlined Saturn 5, and the smooth, cone-shaped Apollo command module, the lunar module is the ugly duckling of the Apollo mission.

There were reasons for the lunar module's strange shape. It was built entirely for flight in outer space—from the orbiting Apollo down to the moon, and then back up again, from the moon to rejoin Apollo. It never had to fly through the air, so it did not need a sleek, streamlined shape. During the launch phase, it would ride in a protective aluminum shell. After its mission on and around the airless, low-gravity moon, it was to be left in space.

So, the landing bug was built in a form that best fitted its mission. Since its mission was to land on the moon and spring off again, it was most practical to build it as a squat object with legs. Its squat shape would make it very steady as it landed, and its springy legs would cushion the landing. Then, when it was time for the two astronauts to leave the moon and join the Apollo, the landing bug would blast off into space once more. But, its lower half, including its legs, would no longer be needed. So, they would be left standing on the moon like the shed husk of a gigantic insect.

From the crew compartment of the bug, the astronauts could

President John F. Kennedy set the course for our space program in 1961 when he announced that the United States would attempt to land men on the moon "before this decade is out." Within less than a year astronaut John H. Glenn, Jr., became the first American to orbit the earth. Astronaut Glenn is shown here after his orbital flight presenting a "hard hat" to the President in an informal ceremony. The hat is a standard piece of safety headgear worn by anyone working around the tall rocket-launch towers of Cape Kennedy.

The original seven Mercury astronauts in their space suits became familiar figures to the nation as the space program developed. These first American spacemen, chosen after exhaustive tests of their stamina and skill, were Alan B. Shepard, Jr., Virgil I. Grissom, L. Gordon Cooper, Walter M. Shirra, Jr., Donald K. Slayton, John H. Glenn, Jr., and M. Scott Carpenter. Because of an unusual heart condition, Slayton was ruled out of space flight but stayed in the program. Grissom was killed in a fire aboard Apollo during ground testing. Carpenter transferred to underwater experimental work after making an orbital flight.

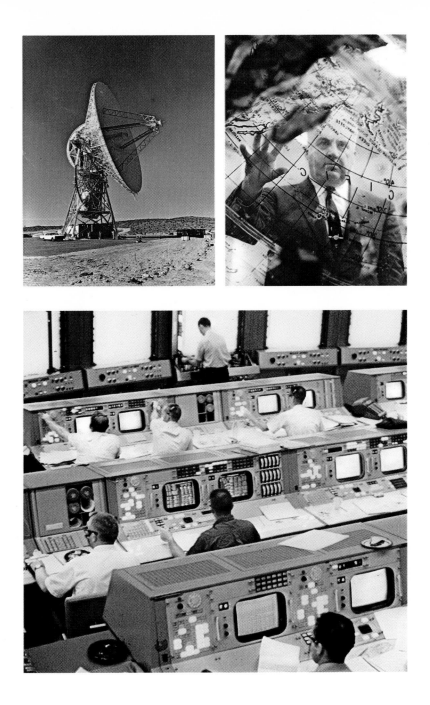

Radar tracking and communications stations were set up around the world to follow the manned space flights. Mission Control Center (bottom photo) was established at the space center in Houston to monitor every action of the rockets, capsules, and astronauts for most of the Gemini and all of the Apollo missions.

Edward H. White was the first American to walk in space. White is shown here against the dramatic backdrop of the earth as he floats outside the orbiting Gemini 4 space ship. White was attached to the space ship by an umbilical cord which provided life support and prevented his drifting away from the ship. The astronaut maneuvered around the ship with the aid of a hand-held gas-firing jet gun. At the right of the picture is the open hatch of the space ship.

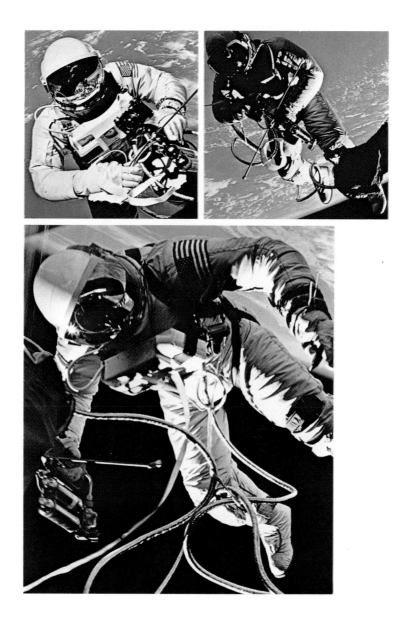

Later Gemini missions further tested space suits outside the capsules, as well as man's ability to perform useful tasks in space.

Gemini ships 6 and 7 achieved the first space rendezvous. Gemini 6 pursued Gemini 7 for 100,000 miles at a speed of 17,000 miles per hour until the two ships came within a foot of one another at an orbiting altitude of 185 miles above the earth. The feat was hailed as the most important step after John Glenn's orbital flight.

Eugene Cernan (right) and Thomas Stafford (not pictured) were scheduled to dock their Gemini 9 with an unmanned Agena, but the protective shroud of the Agena failed to break free and the maneuver was not attempted. Stafford described the Agena as looking like "an angry alligator." Astronaut Charles P. Conrad (left), accompanied by Richard F. Gordon, achieved the docking maneuver in Gemini 11. They fired the Agena engine to boost their ship into an orbit of 850 miles out from the earth, the farthest man had ventured at that time.

This time exposure of the downward swing of the launch tower shows the action as a Titan rocket blasts off. Titan was the launch vehicle for Gemini flights.

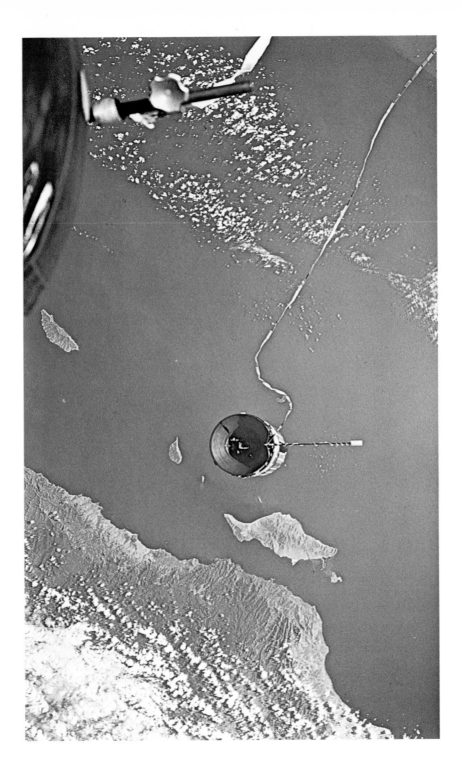

An Agena docking target attached to a Gemini capsule in orbit.

John W. Young smiles up at a recovery helicopter after the successful first flight of Gemini. Young and Virgil I. Grissom put their capsule down in the water, where teams of frogmen attached flotation
collars to insure that the capsule stayed upright and afloat. The astro-

nauts were then hoisted aboard helicopters and flown to waiting recovery ships. On an early Mercury mission with Grissom aboard, a hatch blew open too soon and the capsule sank before rescue teams could secure it. Grissom barely managed to escape.

The first Apollo crew died in a fire aboard the space ship during ground tests January 27, 1967. Virgil I. Grissom was a veteran of both Mercury and Gemini missions. Edward White was the first American to walk in space during the flight of Gemini 4. Roger B. Chaffee was scheduled to make his first flight. The fire apparently started in electrical wiring and swept through the cockpit with furnace-like intensity, fed by the pure oxygen atmosphere inside the spacecraft. An investigation blamed thoughtlessly placed wiring, haphazardly placed combustible materials scattered throughout the cockpit, the pure oxygen the men were breathing, and a cumbersome escape hatch. Modifications and safety precautions made later Apollos much safer, but the program nearly stalled as a result of the tragedy.

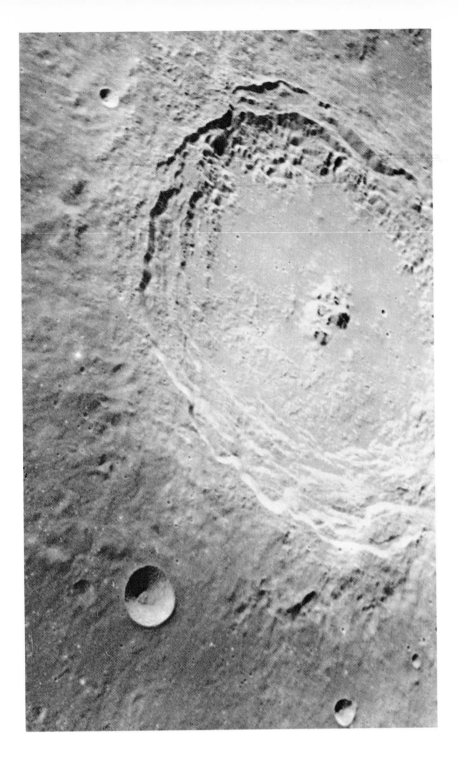

Pictures of Langrenus and other craters taken by unmanned satellites and by early Apollo flights were used to determine the best landing sites for the ultimate touchdown on the moon.

Saturn 5 blasts off. The rocket with Apollo spacecraft stands 363 feet high, and its first stage develops 7.5 million pounds of thrust. The second and third stages develop 1,125,000 pounds and 225,000 pounds respectively. The Saturn Apollo is taller than the Statue of Liberty and weighs well over 6 million pounds.

Views of the earth as seen from Apollo 8 as it sped on its way to orbit the moon. Astronauts Frank Borman, James A. Lovell, Jr., and William A. Anders were the first space travelers to watch the earth receding into the distance in just this way. Even at 207,000 miles away the men could identify seas and land masses.

Apollo 9 tested the lunar module in earth orbit and performed rendezvous maneuvers like those which would be used in preparation for the moon landing. Aboard the lunar module were James A. McDivitt and Russell L. Schweickart, while David R. Scott handled the command module. The photo at top left shows Schweickart outside the LM. The lower left photo is of the lunar module still covered with an aluminum shroud used in the launching phase. At the right, the legs of the LM are extended and it is ready to descend.

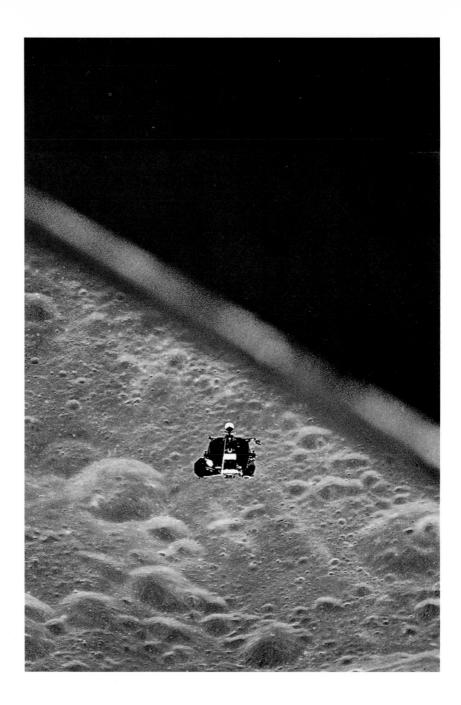

A rainbow-like reflection from within the command ship highlights this picture of the LM on its way toward the moon in the "near miss" mission of Apollo 10, flown by Stafford, Cernan, and John W. Young. In this final mission before the moon landing, Stafford and Cernan took their LM within 50,000 feet of the lunar surface.

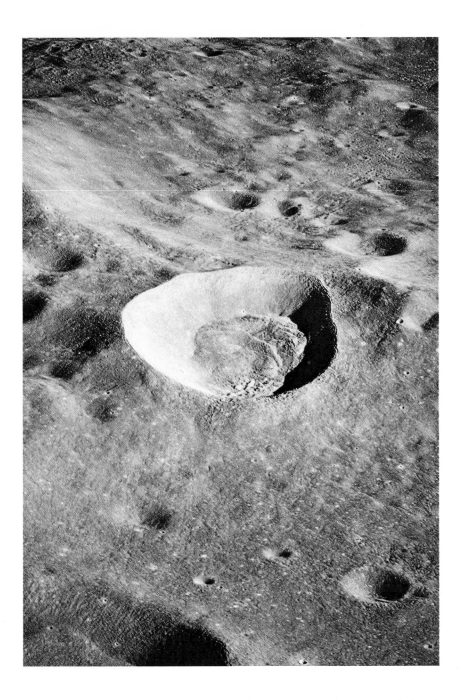

Close-up photographs of ridges and craters on the moon helped establish the lunar landing site.

July 20, 1969, men stand on the surface of the moon. Astronaut Edwin E. Aldrin, Jr., walks on the fine sand of the moon, the life support system on his back and his space suit protecting him from the airless void. He stands near the foil-sheathed landing leg of the LM.

Aldrin plants a solar wind collector to obtain information about emissions from the sun.

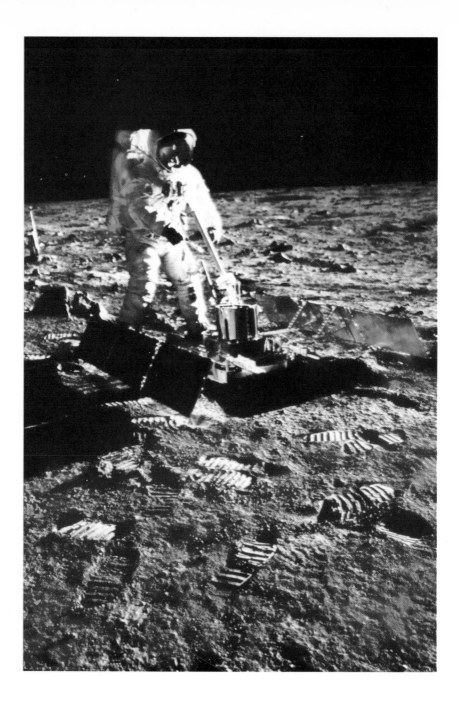

Away from the LM, Aldrin sets up the Passive Experiments package, which included a seismometer to record any moon tremors caused by meteorites, volcanic eruptions, or quakes in the moon's surface.

Also included in the experiments was a two-foot square laser reflector which would reflect a beam of light directly back to earth.
The travel time of the light beam would indicate subtle changes in
earth-moon distances.

Aldrin's face plate reflects a view of the LM and of Neil Armstrong, who took the picture.

Aldrin eases down the ladder to make the last step that will place him on the moon after a four-day journey through space.

Neil A. Armstrong places his foot where no man had walked before.

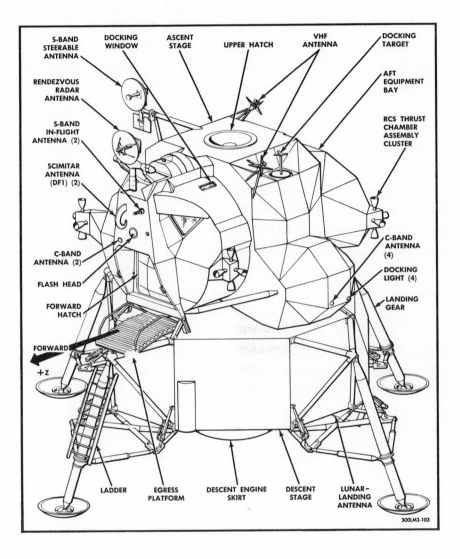

S-BAND
STEERABLE
ANTENNA

DOCKING
WINDOW

ASCENT
STAGE

UPPER HATCH

VHF
ANTENNA

DOCKING
TARGET

RENDEZVOUS
RADAR
ANTENNA

AFT
EQUIPMENT
BAY

S-BAND
IN-FLIGHT
ANTENNA (2)

RCS THRUST
CHAMBER
ASSEMBLY
CLUSTER

SCIMITAR
ANTENNA
(DF1) (2)

C-BAND
ANTENNA
(4)

C-BAND
ANTENNA (2)

DOCKING
LIGHT (4)

FLASH HEAD

LANDING
GEAR

FORWARD
HATCH

FORWARD

+Z

LADDER

EGRESS
PLATFORM

DESCENT ENGINE
SKIRT

DESCENT
STAGE

LUNAR–
LANDING
ANTENNA

300LM3-103

look out through a pair of triangular windows. To save weight, there were no seats for the men; they would stand, loosely harnessed by straps. In front and on either side of them were the control panels for the LM's guidance, communications, environment, and propulsion systems. Above the commander's position, on the left side, was a window through which he could look to steer the bug back for the rendezvous and docking with the command module. At the astronauts' feet was the 42-inch-square forward hatch through which they would leave the bug to walk on the moon's surface.

COMMAND MODULE

Sometimes called merely the Apollo, the command module was a much roomier capsule than either the one-man Mercury or the two-man Gemini. Being inside the Mercury was like being inside a telephone booth. The Gemini was about as roomy as the front seat of a small foreign car. The inside of the Apollo capsule was about as big as the inside of a station wagon.

The cone-shaped capsule was 10 feet 7 inches high and 12 feet 10 inches in diameter at its widest point, which was its blunt end. Its inside was to be a control center, office, kitchen, bedroom, and bathroom for three men for an entire flight, except for the time when two of the men would be in the lunar module for the descent to the moon. The command module's walls were lined with a fantastically complicated instrument panel and consoles, and its cupboards held many kinds of equipment, as well as their food, water, clothing, and waste disposal facilities.

Crewmen would spend most of their time in the three contour couches. The astronaut in the left-hand couch was the spacecraft commander who would usually operate the spacecraft's controls. In the center couch was the command module pilot. He would often work in a well in front of his couch, where he could operate the sextant and telescope for navigation sightings. On the moon trip, he would be the astronaut who would be left behind in the command module while the other two men went to the moon's surface. The astronaut in the right-hand couch was the landing bug's pilot, and his main task would be to check the spacecraft systems—the electricity and oxygen supplies, the fuel system, and the radio and television lines to earth.

SPACECRAFT COMPARED

	MERCURY	GEMINI	APOLLO 7
LENGTH	9 ft. 6 in.	19 ft.	34 ft. 9 in.
BASE DIAMETER	6 ft. 6 in.	10 ft.	12 ft. 10 in.
HABITAL VOLUME	50 cubic ft.	80 cubic ft.	210 cubic ft.
LAUNCH WEIGHT	3,649 lbs.	8,360 lbs.	41,358 lbs.

Apollo was different from Mercury and Gemini in one other way. In Apollo, the astronauts could get up and move around. With the center couch folded, two astronauts could stand at the same time. Two men could sleep in sleeping bags hung hammock-like below the couches.

The command module had five windows: two side windows, two "rendezvous" windows, and a hatch window. The side windows were placed beside the left and the right couches for the purpose of photography and observation. The triangular rendezvous windows, about 8 by 13 inches, were at the ends of the left and right couches. The command module pilot would look through them to steer the module to its rendezvous and link-up with the landing bug.

Toward the narrow end of the cone-shaped module was the tunnel that the two moon-bound astronauts would crawl through to get in and out of the attached landing bug.

docking probe

COMMAND
MODULE

main parachute
(I of 3)

forward boost
protective cover

forward compartment
(earth-landing equipment)

main display
console

side hatch
(quick opening)

AFT boost
protective cover

electrical power
system, space
radiator panel

AFT compartment
(tanks, reaction control
engines, wiring, plumbing

fuel cells (3)

helium tank

reaction control
engines

SERVICE
MODULE

fuel tanks

cryogenic
storage tanks

reaction control
system panel

oxidizer tanks

VHF scimitar
antenna (I of 2)

environmental
control system
space radiator panel

service propulsion
system fuel tanks

AFT bulkhead

service propulsion
engine

S-band high-gain
antenna

AFT bulkhead
heat shield

service propulsion
engine nozzle

SERVICE MODULE

The service module was the section of Apollo beneath the blunt end of the command module. No men would ever ride in it. It would never reach the moon and would be jettisoned just before re-entry to earth. The service module would hold the main rocket for the spacecraft, the rocket fuel, and most of the supplies—oxygen, water, and electrical power units. The service module was just as wide as the command module but more than twice as long —24 feet 2 inches. Its relatively simple structure consisted of a center section or tunnel running the length of the cylinder surrounded by six pie-shaped sections. The supplies and electrical power units would be inside these sections.

In the center was the main rocket. It was a restartable engine, with a bell-shaped nozzle jutting out the rear end of the service module, that could blast with a force of 20,500 pounds. This rocket would take the ship into and out of lunar orbit.

LAUNCH ESCAPE SYSTEM

For a short time after lift-off, the Apollo spacecraft would carry a framework tower rising above the command module's nose. This was the 33-foot-high launch escape tower. Its 147,000-pound thrust rocket was ready, on command, to fire and pull the command module away from the rest of the spacecraft and the Saturn 5 in case of serious trouble. The rocket would shoot the command module and the three astronauts out to sea and safety. In the event all went well with the launching, the escape tower would be jettisoned and allowed to fall back into the sea.

U.S. SPACE ROCKETS
COMPARED

CHAPTER 8

Astronauts Fly the Saturn-Apollo

The time came, at last, when the Saturn-Apollo was ready for manned flight. Four bold missions were carried out by astronauts as they tested the ship in space between the earth and the moon. These missions were beautiful, precision tests that paved the way for the Apollo 11 moon trip.

APOLLO 7

Apollo 7 was a test of the moonship in an orbit around the earth. The launch date was October 11, 1968. The astronauts were Walter Schirra, Donn F. Eisele, and Walter Cunningham.

The first two days of the mission were crammed with tests of the ship's electrical, navigational, propulsion, and control systems. The Saturn booster had been jettisoned, and was still in orbit. Schirra used the orbiting booster as a target for rendezvous maneuvers. A major objective of the mission was to perform eight firings of the Apollo engine, and all eight went perfectly, sometimes kicking the astronauts into an orbit as high as 277 miles, but always giving them a powerful kick. Once, firing the big 20,500-pound-thrust service module rocket, Schirra exclaimed: "Yaba daba doo! That was a ride and a half."

There were some small problems on board the Apollo 7. One instrument gave a false warning on the ship's oxygen flow. Also, some faulty switches temporarily shut down part of the ship's electrical system. Some of the foods brought complaints from the astronauts as being too sweet, and the water often tasted too much of chlorine. For several days the crew, especially Wally Schirra,

APOLLO GUIDANCE AND CONTROL SYSTEM

battled plain old-fashioned head colds. Schirra had a very bold, independent way of skippering his ship. He canceled the first of Apollo 7's planned telecasts from orbit and several times sharply questioned orders from ground controllers.

But as Apollo 7 settled down to the routine of its long flight, the telecasts came to be highlights of each day. They ran about 7 to 11 minutes as the spacecraft passed over tracking stations at Corpus Christi, Texas, and Cape Kennedy. The *Wally, Walt, and Donn Show,* as it was nicknamed, was the first successful live telecast from American astronauts. The astronauts held up crudely lettered signs that read "Hello from the lovely Apollo Room, high above everything." In these television broadcasts, the world caught some brief, inside glimpses of life aboard an orbiting spacecraft.

After 163 almost flawless orbits of the earth, logging more than 4 million miles and taking hundreds of photographs of earth and the eye of a hurricane, the Apollo 7 astronauts rode their command module down to a splashdown October 22 in the choppy

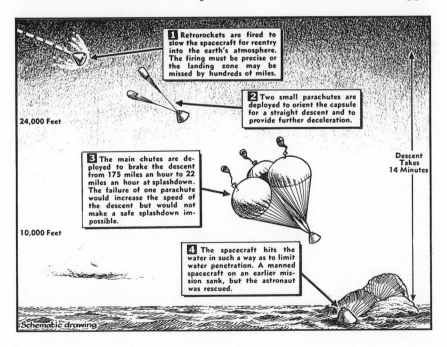

1 Retrorockets are fired to slow the spacecraft for reentry into the earth's atmosphere. The firing must be precise or the landing zone may be missed by hundreds of miles.

2 Two small parachutes are deployed to orient the capsule for a straight descent and to provide further deceleration.

24,000 Feet

Descent Takes 14 Minutes

3 The main chutes are deployed to brake the descent from 175 miles an hour to 22 miles an hour at splashdown. The failure of one parachute would increase the speed of the descent but would not make a safe splashdown impossible.

10,000 Feet

4 The spacecraft hits the water in such a way as to limit water penetration. A manned spacecraft on an earlier mission sank, but the astronaut was rescued.

Schematic drawing

waters south of Bermuda. The swells tipped the spacecraft over, but the crew quickly inflated air bags to right the vehicle so that its apex with the antenna was pointed upward. Soon the astronauts were aboard the recovery ship.

APOLLO 8

Apollo 8 was a test in which an Apollo moonship was put into orbit around the moon. The astronauts who went on this trip were the first men to travel into deep space beyond an earth orbit. They were Frank Borman, James A. Lovell, Jr., and William A. Anders. The launch was on December 21, 1968, shooting the Apollo far out through space and, at last, into orbit around the moon.

As the astronauts came around the eastern edge of the moon, traveling westward near the equator, the sun was shining high overhead. Most of the moon's back side and the eastern edge of the side facing earth were in sunlight. Much of the center part of the moon's face was partly illuminated by earthshine.

One of the first major lunar features the astronauts spotted was Langrenus, one of the many craters with peaks rising from the center of their floors. They next flew over the broad plain called the Sea of Fertility. When asked by ground controllers what "the old moon looks like," Lovell began describing the sights unfolding below:

"The moon is essentially gray, no color. Looks like plaster of paris or sort of grayish beach sand. We can see quite a bit of detail. The Sea of Fertility doesn't stand out as well here as it does back on earth. There's not as much contrast between that and the surrounding craters. The craters are all rounded off. There's quite a few of 'em. Some of them are newer. Many of them look like—especially the round ones—look like they were hit by meteorites or projectiles of some sort. Langrenus is quite a huge crater. It's got a central cone to it. The walls of the craters are terraced, about six or seven different terraces on the way down."

By then Apollo 8 had passed over much of the daytime areas of the moon and was reaching the Sea of Tranquility, an even broader plain on the right side of the moon as seen from earth. With the sun lower, close to the horizon, the astronauts were able to make out more details and their perception of depth and height on the lunar surface was enhanced. This was the way they wanted it. For, on the Sea of Tranquility, lay one of the five sites being considered for the manned lunar landing.

"It's about impossible to miss," Lovell assured the flight controllers. "Very easy to pick out."

The spacecraft then passed over the terminator—the point where daylight changes to darkness. The view in that area, the astronauts reported, was quite sharp. But beyond, even with the earthshine, it became more and more difficult to make out any landmarks.

After moving around the back side and reappearing in their second orbit, the astronauts aimed their 4½-pound television camera toward the moon and transmitted pictures, beginning at 7:29 A.M. It was the first of two television broadcasts from the vicinity of the moon that were seen not only at the Houston control center but in millions of homes throughout the world—wherever people had television sets.

Throughout their orbit, the astronauts gave many of the small, unnamed craters on the back side the names of friends and associates. They even named three for themselves. The craters they named Borman, Lovell, and Anders lie just south of the equator, near where the back of the moon ends and the front begins. Apollo officials said that the crater names were in no way official, merely handy labels to identify some nameless features.

During the telecast, Anders, who handled the camera, described the scene below: "The color of the moon looks like a very whitish gray, like dirty beach sand with lots of footprints in it."

At the end of the second complete orbit, when Apollo 8 was once more behind the moon, its main rocket refired. This dropped the spacecraft from an egg-shaped orbit to a circular orbit nearly 70 miles above the lunar surface.

While orbiting the moon, the astronauts became the first men to witness a lunar sunrise and found it a strange and unexpected experience. According to Lovell, about two minutes before sunrise, a fine white haze appeared over the horizon of the moon, where the sun was about to appear. "It takes a fan shape," he said, "unlike the sunrise on earth, where the atmosphere affects it."

At about 9:30 P.M. on Christmas Eve, the astronauts began their second and last television show from lunar orbit. It ran about 30 minutes and showed the bright moon, in a pitch-black sky, outside the spacecraft window. Borman, describing the moon as a "vast, lonely and forbidding sight," added that it was "not a very inviting place to live or work." Lovell saw the earth as a "grand oasis in the big vastness of space."

As the Christmas Eve telecast neared its end, Borman radioed, "Apollo 8 has a message for you." While the camera showed a view of the craters and mountains of the moon, Anders read the first words from the Book of Genesis:

> In the beginning, God created the heaven and earth.
> And the earth was without form, and void; and darkness was upon the face of the deep . . .

Lovell then took up with the verse beginning,

> And God called the light Day, and the darkness He called Night.

Borman closed the reading with the verse that read:

And God called the dry land Earth, and the gathering together of the waters called He Seas: and God saw that it was
good.

After that, Borman signed off, saying:

Good-by, good night. Merry Christmas. God bless all of you,
all of you on the good earth.

RETURN TO EARTH

After orbiting the moon 10 times in about 20 hours, Apollo
8 headed back toward earth early Christmas morning. It fired its
main rocket engine at 1:10 A.M. to kick out of lunar orbit and
begin the 57-hour coasting voyage toward a splashdown in the
Pacific Ocean.

Once again, tension had gripped everyone in the control room
at Houston. For the rocket firing took place when the spacecraft
was directly behind the moon, out of radio contact with earth. If
the rocket failed to fire, the astronauts of Apollo 8 would remain
in lunar orbit, doomed to die when their oxygen supply ran out.
It was about 15 minutes before flight controllers got word that all
was well.

Through a distance of 231,000 miles, as Apollo 8 swung
around from behind the moon and started for earth, Lovell broadcast the good news, saying these words: "Please be informed there
is a Santa Claus." The Apollo rocket on which the astronauts'
lives depended had fired perfectly.

The astronauts again went on live television to show how they
ate and exercised and how they guided and controlled their 33-
foot-long ship. At the time, Apollo 8 was traveling 2,929 miles an
hour toward earth, 191,750 miles away.

Inside the cabin, Borman was seated in the commander's

couch at the left side. Anders, the cameraman and systems engineer, was working by his couch at the right side. In the middle, Lovell's couch was folded back and he was lying suspended in a weightless condition in the middle of the cabin. His head was out of sight down in the lower equipment bay. His feet could be seen strapped to a wall to keep him from floating around.

All three astronauts wore their soft strap-on hats, equipped with microphones and earphones. They called them their "Snoopy hats," after the comic-strip beagle who often imagines he is a daring World War I fighter pilot. Instead of the bulky pressure suits worn for the lift-off, they wore the more comfortable flight coveralls made of light-weight Beta cloth, a fire-resistant material. On their feet were soft bootie-like boots.

Lovell moved into the equipment area to demonstrate how the astronauts took their exercise. Lying on his back, he pulled two stretchable cords attached to a well near his feet. "He's working with an exercise device that's designed to keep the muscles in shape," explained Borman, the narrator.

Anders prepared some hot cocoa. He cut a tip of the cocoa bag open with scissors and squirted five ounces of hot water into it with a pistol-like injector. Each squeeze released one-half ounce. Then Anders passed the bag to another astronaut. And for good measure, he handed over bags of sugar cookies, orange drink, corn chowder, chicken and gravy, and "a little napkin to wipe your hands when you're done."

Borman described what Anders was doing to prepare some orange drinks: "You can see he's taking the scissors and cutting the plastic end off the little nozzle that he's going to insert the water gun into. And the water's going in. I hope that you'll have better Christmas dinners today than this."

The astronauts, however, had a better meal than that shown on the telecast. It was a TV dinner of real turkey (not dehydrated), cranberry-apple sauce, and a grape drink.

The next television shot showed Lovell at work down in the lower equipment bay that housed his navigation instruments. These included a sextant and scanning telescope with which the astronauts measured the angles from the spacecraft to different target stars and landmarks on the moon. During the day, Lovell made a number of star sightings. "This is where we find out exactly where we are in space, what direction, and how fast we are traveling," he explained. "And our computer takes the information and tells how to maneuver to get home safely."

On December 26, their last full day in space, the astronauts' thoughts turned more and more to earth. During the afternoon telecast, their last of the mission, Anders mused: "I think I must have the feeling that the travelers in the old sailing ships used to have, going on a very long voyage away from home and now we're headed back. I have that feeling of being proud of the trip but still happy to be going back home." The three men spent most of the day carefully checking out their maneuvering rockets, charging batteries, stowing equipment, and dumping waste water in preparation for their return to earth—considered one of the riskiest phases of the mission. Flight controllers cautioned against talking of a successful mission before it was over.

By the time Apollo 8 had reached the upper layers of the atmosphere at about 400,000 feet, the cylindrical service module had already been separated from the cone-shaped command module in which the astronauts were riding. The bolts holding the two modules together were blown away by the firing of small explosive charges.

Shortly after the service module separation, the on-board computer triggered the firing of six thruster rockets to turn the spacecraft's blunt end toward the line of flight. The men were thus riding down backward.

The outer surface of the command module was coated with a plastic, from a half inch to two inches thick on the blunt end.

This coating was a shield against the heat that built up on the command module's outer surface when it slammed against the atmosphere. The material turned white-hot from the friction, charred, and melted away. But, as it melted, it was doing its job —carrying away tremendous amounts of heat so that the inside of the capsule would not get very hot.

The first of a series of three parachute systems opened automatically 8 minutes after re-entry began, when the spacecraft was 23,300 feet above earth. By then, it had slowed to about 300 miles an hour. First to unfold were the two 14-foot-wide drogue chutes, which oriented the craft and continued slowing it. Less than a minute later, Apollo 8 was dropping straight down. Then three small parachutes pulled out the three main parachutes, each 83 feet in diameter. When the nose broke away to let out the parachutes, it exposed a beacon. This flashing white light could be seen from the aircraft carrier Yorktown and the waiting helicopters as Apollo 8 hit the water at about 20 miles an hour—only 4 miles from the Yorktown.

APOLLO 9

Apollo 8 had orbited the moon. But there had been no test of the four-legged lunar module. In fact, the lunar module had not even been carried along on that mission. Instead, tanks of water had been carried, as ballast, to fill in for the weight of the missing craft.

Now, Apollo 9 would test the lunar module in an earth orbit. The men chosen for the mission were James A. McDivitt, David R. Scott, and Russell L. Schweickart. Their goal would be to maneuver the command module and the lunar module separately in orbit, and to bring them together for rendezvous and docking.

The United States was not the only country planning to carry out rendezvous and docking tests in orbit. On January 14, 1969, while preparations were being made for the Apollo 9 mission, the Soviet Union sent two manned Soyuz spacecraft into earth orbit. One pilot was aboard Soyuz 4, launched on January 14. Three men were on Soyuz 5, launched the following day. The two ships joined each other in space and on January 16, two of the three men from Soyuz 5 "walked" outside to transfer from their craft to Soyuz 4. It was the first time men had transferred from one orbiting vehicle to another.

Several weeks later, at 11 A.M. on March 3, the Apollo 9 astronauts rocketed into space. Within 11 minutes after lift-off, they were in orbit. The first two stages of the Saturn 5 had been jettisoned. Therefore, the ship that was in orbit had these parts, beginning at the tail end:

1. The third stage of Saturn 5
2. The Lunar Module, mounted inside a metal casing attached to the Saturn front end
3. The Service Module, including the Apollo rocket engine, just forward of the lunar module
4. The cone-shaped Command Module at the forward end of the ship

The ship was arranged in this way because the command module (where the three astronauts were) had a sleek, streamlined shape that made it a good front end for the launch through the air. But now, out in space, the lunar module had to be moved to the front. It could not be left in back because it would be in the way of the Apollo rocket when it began to blast.

To change the line-up, the two halves of the ship were separated. The service module and command module moved forward, leaving the Saturn third stage and the lunar module behind for the time being. Then Scott turned the command ship through a backward flip and gingerly pulsed small rockets to move 50 feet back for a nose-to-nose link-up with the landing module, still attached to the Saturn.

On the moon landing mission, the Saturn third stage would be used to boost the Apollo out of its earth orbit toward the moon. But, for this test, Apollo was not going to the moon. So, instead, Scott flipped a switch that jettisoned the Saturn third stage in earth orbit. Then, from the ground control center, a signal went to the Saturn computer that made the jettisoned third stage blast far off into an orbit around the sun. The astronauts had maneuvered their craft several thousand feet away by then and could watch the Saturn's spectacular rocket flame. Scott radioed: "It's just like a bright star disappearing in the distance."

After the jettison, all that was left were the three modules of the Apollo. At the back of the command module was the rocket-carrying service module. Together, they formed the main part of the spaceship. Attached to the nose end of this ship was the strange-looking lunar module. A connecting tunnel went between the service module and the lunar module. At each end of the tunnel was a hatch.

On the third day, March 5, the astronauts used that tunnel. Slowed down by bulky, partially inflated spacesuits and oxygen hoses, they removed the command module hatch and reached through the connecting tunnel to open the lunar module hatch. Then Schweickart and later McDivitt crawled through the tunnel (38 inches long and 32 inches wide) into the lunar module. The two men spent nearly 9 hours there, while Scott remained to pilot the command ship. McDivitt and Schweickart switched on nearly all of the lunar module's instruments, extended its four spindly legs, sampled its computer data to make sure it was working well, and ignited the descent engine for a 6-minute firing. They also sent out a short telecast of their activities inside the lunar module cockpit.

The landing module was declared in good shape—which was more than could be said for Schweickart at the time. Twice during these activities, he was hit by severe attacks of nausea, perhaps a form of motion sickness. For a time, flight controllers canceled plans to have Schweickart take a 2-hour space "walk"—called extravehicular activity, or EVA. Though not a high-priority part of the mission, EVA was included to give the astronauts training in the emergency procedure for moving from one vehicle to another if something should block passage through the tunnel or if, on the return from the moon, the two ships were unable to link up when they rendezvoused. It would also provide the first real test of the oxygen-supplying backpack men would use while walking on the moon's surface.

When the astronauts awoke the next day—March 6, their fourth day in orbit—Schweickart had recovered from his nausea and was ready to go EVA in open space.

McDivitt and Schweickart, who had returned to the command module for the night, went back through the tunnel into the lunar module. All three astronauts were fully suited, breathing oxygen piped directly into their suits. The oxygen was let out of both cabins, so that the insides of the modules were complete vacuums, just like the surrounding space. Then hatches on both modules were opened.

Scott stuck his head and shoulders out of the command module hatch to pick up some experiments that had been attached outside. As Apollo 9 soared over the Pacific Ocean at sunrise, Schweickart stepped out on the lunar module's porch-like platform. He spent most of his 40-minute EVA with his booted feet securely planted in a pair of "golden slippers" attached to the porch. These were hard-rubber foot anchors that were covered with gold paint as protection against the sun's intense rays. Being anchored in this way—a lesson learned from the Gemini EVA's—Schweickart could use both hands to operate cameras. "That's what you call a view from the top of the stairs—one stair, that is," Schweickart said.

After Schweickart's EVA, the astronauts shut the hatches and returned to the command module to rest up for their fifth and most critical day in orbit—the day of rendezvous. The rendezvous maneuver was a spectacular display of navigation that lasted for about 6½ hours. McDivitt and Schweickart went back into the lunar module and, when all was ready on Apollo's 59th orbit around the earth, Scott tripped a switch in the command module cockpit to release the twelve latches holding the two ships together at the tunnel.

"Spider" was then free of "Gumdrop." In their radio communications between the two ships, the astronauts referred to the lunar module as Spider, because of its insect-like appearance, and to the command module as Gumdrop, because the cone-shaped vehicle was delivered from the factory to the Cape in a blue, plastic, candy-like wrapping.

After making sure that Spider was working perfectly, McDivitt and Schweickart fired small lunar module rockets to pull their ship away from Scott and Gumdrop. For an hour they drifted within a few miles of Gumdrop, checking out their rendezvous radar and guidance systems. Then McDivitt fired up the lunar module's descent rocket to climb into a 156-mile-high orbit, 13 miles above the command module. "It got a little rough and shaky as I was throttling up," McDivitt reported. The lunar module continued on its course for nearly two hours while the two craft circled the earth, their maximum distance from each other reaching 50 miles.

Then when Spider got back within sight of Gumdrop, McDivitt refired the descent rocket. Shortly afterward, he triggered explosive bolts to jettison the lunar module's lower stage with its four legs, exposing the nozzle of their ascent rocket. When the lunar module, flying higher in an "outside track," fell behind about 100 miles, McDivitt fired the ascent engine the way it would be done at take-off from the moon. With several firings, McDivitt and Schweickart steadily closed the gap between themselves and Gumdrop. If they had failed to find Gumdrop, the two men in Spider would have been stranded in orbit to die when their oxygen supply ran out.

But their radar and rockets worked flawlessly. When the squat, bug-like lunar module hove into view, Scott radioed greetings: "You're the biggest, friendliest, funniest-looking spider I've ever seen."

Finally, coached by Scott, McDivitt slowly brought the lunar module up to the mother ship for the redocking. After McDivitt and Schweickart squeezed back through the tunnel into the command module, the astronauts released the lunar module, and, on a radioed command from the ground, the ascent engine was refired until all of its fuel was gone. Both the descent and ascent stages of the lunar module were now only so much space junk which would burn up as they dipped back into earth's atmosphere several weeks later.

After completing the rendezvous, the Apollo 9 astronauts were left alone in orbit with fully 97 per cent of their mission objectives already completed, but with five more days of flight. They made good use of the time, practicing navigation and tracking skills and conducting photographic experiments designed to study the earth. On March 13, the three astronauts brought their spacecraft to a smooth and accurate splashdown in the Atlantic Ocean north of Puerto Rico. It hit the water less than a mile away from its target point and only three miles north of the waiting recovery ship, the U.S.S. Guadalcanal. Television cameras on the helicopter carrier were able to show the worldwide audience the last moments of the parachute-aided descent and all of the recovery operations by helicopter and frogmen. The men were safe and healthy after ten successful days in space.

APOLLO 10

In May, 1969, the Apollo 10 was launched. Apollo 8 had carried out a moon orbit without taking along the lunar module. Apollo 9 had tested the lunar module, but did not leave earth orbit. Apollo 10 was to combine both of these missions. The astronauts' job was to take the Apollo into a lunar orbit *and* to test the lunar module. They would do everything except make a moon landing. This mission would be the final practice for the Apollo 11 moon trip.

The astronauts chosen for Apollo 10 were Thomas P. Stafford, John W. Young, and Eugene A. Cernan. The three men named their round-ended command module "Charlie Brown," and they named their four-legged lunar module "Snoopy."

A perfect launching sent the three astronauts on their moonward course early on a Sunday afternoon. After circling the earth one and a half times, the Saturn 5's third-stage engine refired for 5 minutes to blast the spaceship out of its low earth orbit at a speed of about 24,200 miles an hour. "We're on the way!" radioed Stafford.

In a maneuver just like the one done for Apollo 9, the astronauts separated their command module from the rest of the "stack," did a back flip, and moved its nose in for a docking with the lunar module, nestled on top of the Saturn 5 third stage. Then, while their color television camera was transmitting, the astronauts pulled the attached lunar module out of its nest and watched the Saturn 5 drop back in the blackness of space.

For three days Apollo 10 and its crew coasted toward the moon, losing speed until, within 38,000 miles of the moon, they were pulled ever faster by the moon's gravity. It was a relaxed time. Some of the problems of the earlier flights, the colds and nausea, were missing. The astronauts' only complaints were too much chlorine in the water, hydrogen bubbles in the water that caused stomach gas, and some drifting snow-like particles of glass fiber from a rip in the command module's hatch covering.

At 4:45 P.M., Eastern Daylight Time, on May 21, Apollo 10's service module rocket fired to slow down the ship and send the astronauts into an orbit of the moon. The astronauts then turned their color television camera on, to give the people back home a 29-minute show of what it was like to fly over the craters of the moon.

Early the next morning, Cernan and Stafford crawled through the connecting tunnel into Snoopy, leaving Young behind in Charlie Brown. After checking all instruments, the two astronauts separated their lunar module from the command module. Then, firing the lunar module's descent rocket, they streaked down through the lunar sky at a speed of 3,700 miles an hour. "We're right there! We're right over it," Cernan called over his radio. "I'm telling you, we are low, we're close, babe. This is it." Snoopy was soaring 47,000 feet above the moon—not much higher than the altitude at which jet airliners fly over the earth.

On Snoopy's first low pass, Stafford looked out the window and described the Apollo landing site in the Sea of Tranquility. He said that it looked "very smooth, like wet clay, like a dry river bed in New Mexico or Arizona." He was able to pick out many details—boulders, small craters, and deep cracks in the moon's surface.

Just before the second fly-over, the two astronauts in Snoopy had a scare. Explosive bolts were automatically triggered to jettison Snoopy's lower stage with its four spindly legs. At that moment the upper stage went into a fast spin, pitching up and down. "Something is wrong with the gyro," shouted Cernan. Stafford took over the hand controls, and after about a minute was able to steady the spacecraft.

Later, NASA engineers decided that a control switch had been left in the wrong position. That mistake had probably been made before the launch, while the lunar module was being checked out.

By the time Snoopy and its pilots had settled down, they were again within 9 miles of the moon. "I'll tell you," Cernan said, "we're down there where we can touch the top of some of the hills." At this time, the lunar module's rocket fired for 15 seconds to boost the two astronauts back toward their rendezvous with the command module. The rocket sent them on an upward curving course like the one astronauts taking off from the moon would follow. As the two spacecraft docked together, one of the astronauts shouted, "Snoopy and Charlie Brown are hugging each other."

After Stafford and Cernan crawled back into Charlie Brown, they closed the hatches and jettisoned the unmanned lunar module upper stage. Its rocket was fired until all the fuel was burned, sending the craft out into a wide orbit of the moon. Cernan said, "That little Snoopy was a real winner."

To hear Stafford describe it, a ride in the lunar module's upper stage was quite an experience. When the smaller rockets were fired for the last seconds of the rendezvous, he said the thin aluminum alloy walls of the vehicle shook and rattled. "If you wanted a Lunar Module . . . ride," Stafford told ground controllers, "let your kids get a big metal bowl on your head and beat on it with spoons."

The Apollo 10 astronauts kept orbiting the moon for another full day. From their orbit, ranging from altitudes of 63 to 75 miles above the moon, they observed craters that looked like volcanoes and others that looked as if they had been caused by meteor collisions. "There's one on the back side," Stafford said, "that if it was in a different setting you would call it Mount Fujiyama." Later, Stafford reported seeing a crater whose outside slope was covered with "so many big, black boulders" that it looked "like a forest of pine trees."

With a powerful push from their spacecraft rocket, the Apollo 10 astronauts broke out of moon orbit early Saturday morning, May 24, and headed for earth with ever-increasing speed. Their aim was true. Their spacecraft was still performing smoothly. They were tired but in good spirits after their 31 orbits around the moon.

Looking back on the scarred face of the moon, Cernan said: "I tell you, this satellite of ours—this moon of ours—had a rough beginning somewhere back there."

Then Apollo 10 went through the same maneuvers that Apollo 8 followed to get back to earth. The service module was jettisoned. An automatic command from the computer fired maneuvering rockets to point the blunt end of the cone-shaped command module toward the earth at an angle. Then, came the fiery re-entry through the air. Finally, the parachutes unfurled and, as dawn came to the South Pacific, Apollo 10 dropped into the water within sight of the U.S.S. Princeton, a helicopter carrier standing by for the recovery.

CHAPTER 9

Men for the Moon

"When ships to sail the void between the stars have been invented," said Johannes Kepler, the German scientist who had so much to do with explaining the motions of bodies in space, "there will also be men who come forward to sail those ships."

The ships have been invented, and out of the 3½ billion people in the world, the 202 million Americans, and the 50 active astronauts, three men were selected to make the first voyage to land on the moon. They had worked together as a team for more than a year. First, as the backup pilots for Apollo 8, they learned through ground training and long textbook study the ways of a Saturn 5 in flight, of a command module on the way to the moon, and of a fiery re-entry to splashdown. Then, since January, 1969, when they were chosen for Apollo 11, they had practiced for weeks on end at the controls of the command module and the lunar module. The two men who would actually land on the moon spent hours learning geology and photography and studying lunar maps to be able to make the most of the short time they would spend on the moon's surface.

What kind of men are these three astronauts who were chosen for the moon trip?

The commander of the Apollo moonship was Neil Armstrong, blond-haired and boyish looking. This modest, somewhat shy man has had a brave and adventurous flying history. As a Navy pilot he flew 78 combat missions off the carrier Essex in the Korean war. On one of these missions, a cable stretched across a North Korean valley sliced off one wing of his jet. He nursed the plane back over friendly territory and bailed out safely. After the Korean war, he continued his college education, getting a degree in aeronautical engineering from Purdue University. More recently, he has flown many missions in the high-speed X-15 experimental plane as a test pilot, and had several close calls.

Neil Armstrong was born on August 5, 1930, in the living room of his grandparents' farmhouse, six miles from the small town of Wapakoneta, Ohio. His love for flying came early in his life. When he was six, he went for a plane ride with his father in a Ford Tri-Motor. The next year, he began to build model airplanes, a hobby that went on for many years. His feelings about flying also showed up in his dreams. In those years, he would often have a dream in which, by holding his breath, he could rise up into the air and hover above the ground.

As a teenager, Armstrong advanced quickly in school, doing especially well in science and math. In high school, he even substituted for his science teacher when the teacher was out ill for a while. His success in school was not all that he was accomplishing —he took flying lessons, and had his pilot's license before he got his driver's license. He worked as a mechanic at an airport, spent time star-gazing through a neighbor's telescope, and built a wind tunnel in the basement of his parents' home in order to test the wing and body shapes of model airplanes. Aviation and outer space fascinated him.

Throughout all his years of flying adventures, Neil Armstrong has remained a quiet, thoughtful man with a dry sense of humor. His preferred way of life is shown by the fact that he and his wife raised their children in a former forest ranger's cabin in the foothills of the San Gabriel Mountains, instead of living in the nearby town of Lancaster, California, where most of the X-15 test pilots lived.

Edwin E. Aldrin, Jr., who goes by the nickname of "Buzz," was the pilot of the Apollo Lunar Module. Buzz Aldrin is a determined man with a very definite manner. He always knows what his goals are and he knows how to go about reaching them. He is a rugged-looking man, his blond hair mostly gone now, who lives vigorously. He goes in for physical exercise and for staying in good condition, and stays in shape by pole vaulting in his back yard.

Aldrin also flew combat missions in the Korean War. In his 66 missions, flying an F-86 Sabrejet, he shot down two MIG 15's and damaged another.

Buzz Aldrin was born January 20, 1930, in Montclair, New Jersey. His father, Colonel Edwin Eugene Aldrin, Sr., was himself an adventurous flyer, steeped in aviation. The father of the future astronaut studied under Robert Goddard, the rocket pioneer, knew one of the Wright brothers who flew the world's first airplane, and he himself set a cross-country flying record in 1929, the year before Buzz was born.

Buzz Aldrin not only inherited his father's love of flying— he also was strongly successful in his studies. He graduated third highest in his class at West Point and later earned a doctor's degree in astronautics at the Massachusetts Institute of Technology. It has been said that he is the best scientific mind that we have sent into space.

Michael Collins was the pilot of the Command Module. Collins, a former Edwards Airforce Base test pilot, is a dark-haired, relaxed man who likes to raise roses in his backyard and who plays a strong game of handball. He is casual and breezy in his manner, a man who shows his feelings openly, and doesn't take himself too seriously.

Mike Collins was born in Rome, Italy, on October 31, 1930. His father, a United States Army general, was stationed in Rome at the time as a military observer. Mike was an active boy, who enjoyed life a great deal, and who was a good athlete. In his teens, he was captain of the wrestling team at St. Albans School for Boys in Washington, D.C. Then, as now, he was warm, popular, and full of spirit.

Mike went to college at West Point, where he graduated in 1952. His grades there had not been especially good. But he had done well enough, even with his relaxed kind of studying, to get his college degree. Next, he joined the Air Force, where he entered test-pilot school. That was the start of the career that led him, finally, to the Apollo 11 launch pad.

These, then, were the three men who took Apollo to the moon. They have many things in common. All are married men with children. All three had already gone into space on Gemini missions. They were the best kind of men that could be found anywhere for this voyage.

CHAPTER 10

Days
of Waiting

Throughout the history of exploration there had never been an expedition planned and prepared with such care as Apollo 11.

The many and highly complex components of the command module, the lunar module, and the Saturn 5 had been tested in a variety of ways, both on the ground and in space. For years men and computers had worked out the mathematics, plotted the course, and studied the risks. Their work had led to ways to keep the spacecraft from getting too hot or too cold, keep it from losing communications with earth, keep its engines from firing too long or too short, and to stay on course at distances of 250,000 miles from its home base. Such careful preparations continued right through those final days of waiting, the days leading up to launching time on July 16.

Early on June 27, launching crews began the Countdown Demonstration Test (CDDT), or the dress rehearsal, for Apollo 11. This included all the steps of the actual countdown, all the tests, the complete fueling of the rocket, the entrance of the astronauts into the spacecraft cabin. A week later, shortly before 9:32 A.M. on July 3, a clear voice came through the intercom at the Firing Room 1: "You're cleared for firing command." In a few seconds, a man wearing a short-sleeved shirt leaned over his control console and pressed the button that initiated the automatic, 3 minute and 7 second sequence of computerized events leading up to lift-off. Without a hitch, the countdown ticked away to the point of ignition. But it was only a make-believe countdown, the final practice for the real thing.

They were practicing for the mission in a dummy model of the Apollo command module, called a simulator. All the dials and gauges, switches, hand controls and computer display panels were just as they are in the real spacecraft.

For nearly eight hours, while instructors operated the four computers that ran the simulator, the astronauts practiced over and over again the first 12 minutes of the flight. There were times when the make-believe lift-off was free of trouble. Other times, to test the astronauts' reflexes and knowledge of the systems and alternate mission plans, the instructors ordered the computers to throw in an error or two.

For the last two months before the flight, each of the astronauts spent more than 400 hours in command module and lunar module simulators at Cape Kennedy and at Houston. It was thus possible to practice every step of the 8-day mission—launching, earth-orbit operations, the rocket firing to leave low earth orbit and head for the moon, the insertion into lunar orbit, the landing on the moon, the lift-off from the moon and, the return to earth.

One of the most unusual simulators, was a real flying vehicle, the lunar landing traning vehicle. It had a nickname—the "Flying Bedstead." But it had much the same pilot-handling characteristics as the lunar module. Undisturbed by an accident earlier in the year, in which Armstrong had to bail out of a crashing trainer, the two moon explorers spent hours piloting the vehicle to soft touchdowns.

All three astronauts also spent long hours learning their mission plan, operating the guidance and navigation computer (which took nearly 40 per cent of their training time), working in a large vacuum chamber at Houston and getting brief sensations of weightlessness during sudden dips in a KC-135 airplane. But in the last few days before lift-off, the three men slowed down their training. They were following their doctors orders. Having in mind the fatigue and illness that delayed Apollo 9 by three days, Charles A. Berry, the astronauts' flight surgeon, ordered the training slowdown and also placed the crew in semi-quarantine for the final two weeks. The men were watched for the slightest symptoms of illness that might hamper the flight. The only people who could come in contact with them were their training associates and their immediate families—so long as they were healthy.

No exceptions could be made even for the President of the United States. After the arrangements were already made for President Nixon to dine with the astronauts on the night before the launch, Berry "suggested" to the White House that, from a medical standpoint, even the President should not be near the astronauts. The dinner was canceled.

Just as the astronauts were waiting for their moon journey, the possibility of "back-contamination" was dramatized in a chilling best-seller, *The Andromeda Strain*. The book was a fictional story about a strain of alien germs brought back to earth from outer space.

The Apollo 11 astronauts were not likely, however, to bring

back some deadly strain. Biologists doubted that the airless moon had any germs or viruses on it. But, early in the Apollo Project, a committee of the National Academy of Sciences had decided that a strict quarantine was a good idea—just in case. This led to NASA's construction of a laboratory with vacuum chambers for the lunar dirt samples and sealed quarters for the astronauts and their doctors, technicians, and cook. That way, even if there were dangerous moon germs, they would not be easily spread around the earth.

Whatever germs the astronauts brought back from the moon, they were not starting their voyage with any signs of illness. On Friday, July 11, they went through a 4-hour medical examination and were pronounced physically fit for flight.

COUNTDOWN

No magic button was pressed, or switch flipped. A master clock in Firing Room 1 simply began ticking at 8 P.M. on Thursday, July 10. As the clock ticked, launching controllers began sending electrical power to the 363-foot-tall moon vehicle at the pad. It was the beginning of the countdown. The days of waiting were now being measured in hours and minutes and seconds.

"WILLING AND READY"

The countdown proceeded smoothly. Rocco Petrone, the launch director, called it the smoothest yet. The crowds at Cocoa Beach waiting to see the launch grew larger. It was hard to believe but it was happening: men were poised to go to the moon.

Two nights before the launching, Armstrong, Aldrin, and Collins made their final public appearances in a nationally televised 30-minute interview. They were asked questions by four newsmen selected from the 3,000 there. Because of the semi-quarantine, the interview was conducted over closed-circuit television. The astronauts, wearing short-sleeved shirts and sitting in soft chairs, were in one building and the newsmen were 15 miles away in another.

Armstrong appeared slightly nervous, choosing his words with care, and Aldrin was stiff and unsmiling. Only Collins appeared relaxed.

Asked if they had any fears about the mission, Armstrong replied: "Fear is not an unknown emotion to us. But we have no fear of launching out on this expedition."

Aldrin told the newsmen that it was all right to use the term "when" and not "if" in referring to the moon landing. "We're thinking positively," he said.

"After a decade of planning and hard work," Armstrong declared, "we're willing and ready to attempt to achieve our national goal."

CHAPTER 11

Four Days to the Moon

"Go, baby, go!" The familiar murmur spread like fire through the control rooms. Only this time they said it with more feeling than usual. On the beaches, they shaded their eyes against the bright sun and held their breaths. Across the land, they paused at their jobs and rushed to television sets.

This was the "big one" at last. It was not just another space flight. This was *the* historic flight to put men on the moon! Could Armstrong and Aldrin really land and walk on the moon? The whole world waited anxiously to find out.

It was July 16, 1969, and the "big one" began on schedule. At 9:32 A.M., E.D.T., orange flames and dark smoke spewed out of the huge Saturn 5 rocket supporting the Apollo 11 spaceship at Cape Kennedy. Then, ever so slowly, the 3,817-ton vehicle struggled to overcome the earth's gravity, finally cleared the Pad 39-A launching tower, and arced out over the Atlantic Ocean.

As the rocket launched Neil Armstrong, Buzz Aldrin, and Mike Collins on their 8-day, 500,000-mile journey, the powerful blast-off made the ground shake. The Apollo 11 streaked upward through a wispy white cloud, in a trail of fire.

President Nixon, who had watched the lift-off on television in Washington, declared a National Day of Participation for the lunar exploration set for four days hence. Urging that Americans be given the day off from work, he said:

"In past ages, exploration was a lonely enterprise. But today, the miracles of space travel are matched by miracles of space communications; even across the vast lunar distance, television brings the moment of discovery into our homes and makes all of us participants. As the astronauts go where man has never gone, as they attempt what man has never tried, we on earth will want, as one people, to be with them in spirit, to share the glory and the wonder and to support them with prayers that all will go well."

And, certainly all Americans, indeed all mankind, felt that they were a part of this history-in-the-making. The astronauts already were carrying with them tokens to be left on the moon. In addition to the metal plaque attached to a leg of the lunar module, the tokens included messages of goodwill from 73 heads of state, a United States flag, and medals honoring the Soviet cosmonauts and American astronauts who have died in the conquest of space.

Actually, for the first four days of the Apollo journey, the world saw little that was new. Moving toward the moon, the three astronauts closely followed a trail already blazed by Apollo 10 two months before. Until the landing craft with Armstrong and Aldrin aboard swooped to within 50,000 feet of the moon where the final descent began, the crew faced challenges and risks that were familiar. They met with no troubles.

During this time, the astronauts performed the routine tasks of a space flight, checking equipment and systems, carrying out everyday housekeeping chores, and conducting regularly scheduled telecasts for the folks back home. From all indications, the men were comfortable and relaxed. "We have a happy home," Collins said during one of the telecasts. "Plenty of room for the three of us. We're all finding our favorite little corners."

On Friday, when Apollo 11 was three-quarters of the way to the moon, Armstrong and Aldrin took a televised inspection tour of the attached lunar module. To do this, they had to open the hatch of the cone-shaped command ship, Columbia, and then squeeze through the 30-inch-wide tunnel into the lunar module, the Eagle. This was the procedure they were to follow later for the actual descent. The telecast, which ran an hour and 36 minutes, was one of the clearest color TV transmissions ever sent from space. Viewers on earth could read dials on the lunar module control panels.

INTO LUNAR ORBIT

The first really anxious moments of the Apollo mission came around noon on Saturday when the linked Columbia and Eagle swung around the leading edge of the moon to begin the transition into lunar orbit. For 33 minutes, the spacecraft was out of radio contact with tracking stations on earth. During that time, the astronauts had to fire the craft's main rocket to slow the vehicle down so that it could be captured by lunar gravity. If the rocket failed to fire, Apollo 11 would loop the moon and head back to earth. If it fired too long, the vehicle could crash into the lunar surface.

But the rocket performed almost flawlessly. When the spaceship swept into moon orbit, Armstrong broke the tense silence at last: "It was like perfect," he reported.

But everything up to now was really only warm-up for the highly complex descent of Eagle to the lunar surface—the encounter with the unknown. Here was a challenge which men had never tackled before. During a time of little more than 10 minutes, Armstrong and Aldrin had to sweep about 300 miles across the face of the moon in their lunar module, descending on a long curve from 50,000 feet to touchdown. A major equipment failure or a miscalculation could mean turning back from the goal or, in the final phase, disaster. If one of the landing craft's spindly legs broke upon landing because of boulders or an unexpected movement, or if the touchdown happened on a steep slope, the craft could tip over and the astronauts would be unable to lift off for a return trip.

The descent procedure began on the Apollo's thirteenth moon orbit after Armstrong and Aldrin had crawled into the lunar module, leaving Collins to fly the command module. The two ships broke their link and drew apart. "How does it look?" Mission Control asked Armstrong. "Eagle has wings," he replied.

Armstrong and Aldrin rode the Eagle back around to the moon's far side where the descent engine was to fire in order to send the module toward the moon on a long, curving course. Suspense built up in the control room at Houston because once again the astronauts were out of radio touch with the ground.

Armstrong finally broke the suspense with a calm report: "The burn was on time." In the command module, Collins reported to Mission Control, "Listen, baby, things are going just swimmingly, just beautiful."

When Armstrong and Aldrin reached 50,000 feet from the moon's surface, green lights on the computer display keyboard blinked the number 99. This signaled Armstrong that he had 5 seconds to decide whether to go ahead for the landing or return to the command module. The ship commander pressed the "proceed" button.

The engine built up thrust gradually, firing as the lunar module headed toward the moon. Seven minutes after the firing, the astronauts, riding upside down according to flight plan, were 21,000 feet above the surface and moving toward the landing site. The guidance computer was driving the rocket engine. At 7,200 feet, with the landing site about 5 miles ahead, the computer ordered maneuvers to tilt the bug-shaped craft almost upright. Armstrong and Aldrin then got their first close-up view of the plain they were aiming for.

The brownish-gray land rushed below them—the craters, hills, and ridges, deep cracks and ancient rubble of the moon. Their target was in the Sea of Tranquility, one of five smooth landing sites that had been selected along the lunar equator on the basis of pictures taken by unmanned spacecraft. Being on the equator reduces the maneuvering required for the astronauts to get there. The sites were on the side of the moon always facing earth; this, of course, made it possible to communicate with the explorers.

The Eagle closed in on the target, dropping about 20 feet a second until it was hovering almost directly over the selected landing spot at an altitude of 500 feet. Then came a startling blow: the floor was littered with boulders. Armstrong quickly grabbed manual control. As he said later, "The auto-targeting was taking us right into a football-field-sized crater, with a large number of boulders and rocks."

Armstrong retained partial control of the module for the rest of the way down. The computer controlled the rocket firing, but the astronaut could adjust the craft's hovering position. For about 90 seconds, Armstrong searched for a clear spot; finally he found one that he liked. Slowly the craft eased down until a blue light on the cockpit flashed to signal that 5-foot-long probes, like curb feelers, on the legs had touched the surface.

"Houston, Tranquility Base here. The Eagle has landed."

"Roger, Tranquility," ground control replied. "We copy you on the ground. You got a bunch of guys about to turn blue. We are breathing again. Thanks a lot."

Although Armstrong is known as a man of few words, his heartbeats told of his excitement upon leading man's first landing on the moon. At the time of the descent rocket ignition, his heartbeat rate registered 110 a minute—77 is normal for him—and it shot up to 156 at touchdown.

The landing actually was 4 miles down range—meaning 4 miles too far to the west—but it was well within the planned area. When they landed, the astronauts were not sure exactly where they were.

Mission Control immediately reported the landing to Collins, who was riding the command ship Columbia about 65 miles overhead. 'Yea, I heard the whole thing," replied the man who went so far but not all the way. "Fantastic."

Yes, fantastic! They had done it! By flying their craft to the lunar surface and landing there, by conquering this great unknown, Armstrong and Aldrin had proved that the moon was now within man's reach. The next step, the true purpose of this fantastic mission, was to sample the unknown, to walk on the moon and learn how safe or unsafe it was for man.

CHAPTER 12

On the Moon

At 10:56 P.M., E.D.T., on July 20, 1969, Neil A. Armstrong stepped into history. From the bottom rung of the ladder leading down from Apollo 11's landing craft, he reached out his booted left foot and planted the first human footprint on the moon.

Then he said the long-awaited words that are sure to be written in history books: "That's one small step for a man, one giant leap for mankind."

There it was, man meeting moon. For explorers, it was the realization of centuries of dreams. For scientists, it meant a chance for possible clues to the origin and nature of both the moon and the earth.

Armstrong was able to share the triumphal moment with man-

kind. Through the miracle of modern communications, hundreds
of millions of people on earth—probably the largest audience ever
—witnessed the astronaut's first step over TV and heard his words
on radio. It took just 1.3 seconds, the time it takes for radio waves
to travel the 238,000 miles between moon and earth, for Armstrong's image to appear on home screens. This gave viewers a
feeling of "I was there" when history was made.

What was this new world like, this remote space frontier suddenly invaded by man? Earlier, looking through the windows of
the landing craft, Armstrong and his crewmate, Buzz Aldrin, radioed this first impression of the general area in which they
touched down:

> [There is a] level plain cratered with a fairly large number
> of craters of the 5- to 50-foot variety. And some ridges, small,
> 20 to 30 feet high, I would guess. And literally thousands of
> little one- and two-foot craters around the area. We see some
> angular blocks out several hundred feet in front of us that
> are probably two feet in size and have angular edges. There
> is a hill in view just about on the ground track ahead of us.
> Difficult to estimate, but might be half a mile or a mile . . .
> I'd say the color of the local surface is very comparable to
> that we observed from orbit at this sun angle—about 10 de-
> grees sun angle or that nature. It's pretty much without color.
> It's gray and it's very white as you look into the zero phase
> line. And it's considerably darker gray, more like an ashen
> gray, as you look out 90 degrees to the sun. Some of the sur-
> face rocks in close here that have been fractured or dis-
> turbed by the rocket engine plume are coated with this light
> gray on the outside. But where they've been broken, they dis-
> play a dark, very dark, gray interior and it looks like it could
> be country basalt.

When Armstrong reached the bottom of the lunar module's
ladder, he said: "The surface is fine and powdery. I can pick it

up loosely with my toe. It does adhere in fine layers like powdered charcoal to the sole and sides of my boots. I only go in a small fraction of an inch, maybe an eighth of an inch. But I can see the footprints of my boots and the treads in the fine sandy particles."

Then, while the excited audience watched those first few moments in awe, Armstrong began to walk carefully across the

LIFE SUPPORT SYSTEM

surface. He found that he could move about easily in his bulky white spacesuit and heavy backpack while under the influence of lunar gravity, which makes everything weigh only one-sixth of what it weighs on earth.

After 19 minutes, Armstrong was joined outside the landing craft by Aldrin, who had been preparing and handing down equipment for the two hours of probing and experimenting.

As Aldrin came through the hatch and started down the ladder, he said, "I want to back up and partially close the hatch, making sure not to lock it on my way out."

"Good thought," Armstrong agreed.

"That's our home for the next couple of hours," Aldrin added. "We want to take good care of it."

Then, as Aldrin started his first testing of the surface, Armstrong said: "Isn't this fun?"

"Right in this area I don't think there's much fine powder," Aldrin said. "It's hard to tell whether it's a clod or a rock."

"You can pick it up," Armstrong pointed out.

"And it bounces," was Aldrin's answer.

They immediately set up another TV camera away from the craft to give people on earth a broader look at the Sea of Tranquility landscape: a bleak, empty, almost flat, crater-pocked surface. Yet, Armstrong described the landscape as having "a stark beauty all its own."

"It's like much of the high desert of the United States," he said. "It's different but it's very pretty out here."

One of the first things the astronauts did was to plant their 3-by-5-foot American flag. It was stiffened with thin wire so as to appear to be flying on the windless lunar surface.

WALKING LIKE KANGAROOS

The astronauts found walking and working on the moon less

tiring than had been predicted. Armstrong once reported he was "very comfortable." Even with their heavy spacesuits and backpacks, the men bounded about easily in kangaroo, almost floating hops. "You do have to be rather careful to keep track of where your center of mass is," Aldrin observed after testing his agility. "Sometimes it takes about two or three paces to make sure that you've got your feet underneath you," he explained. "And about two to three, or maybe four, easy paces can bring you to a fairly smooth stop. Like a football player, you just have to put out to the side and cut a little bit. The so-called kangaroo hop—it does work, but it seems the forward ability is not quite as good as it is in the more conventional one foot after another. As far as saying what a safe pace might be—the one that I'm using now could get rather tiring after several hundred. But this may be a function of the suit as well as lack of gravity forces."

Aldrin discussed the problem of seeing into the dark shadows: "I've noticed several times in going from the sunlight into shadow that just as I go in I catch an additional reflection off the LEM that, along with reflection of my face into the visor, makes visibility very poor just as the transition of sunlight into shadow. Since we have so much glare coming onto my visor—shadow—and then it takes a short while for my eyes to adapt to the lighting conditions. Inside the shadow area, visibility is, as we said before, not too great. But with both visors up we can certainly see what sort of footprints we have and the condition of the soil. Then after being out in the sunlight a while it takes . . . watch it, Neil. Neil, you're on a cable. Yeah, lift up your right foot. Right foot. It's still hooked on it. Wait a minute. Okay, you're clear now."

It was an eerie scene, like a throwback to Buck Rogers science fiction. The black-and-white TV pictures of the lunar module and the astronauts were so sharp and clear as to seem unreal, more like a toy and toy-like figures than human beings on the most daring and far-reaching expedition thus far undertaken.

At one point the astronauts were suddenly interrupted by a summons from Houston. Then President Nixon came on a tele-phone-radio hookup to congratulate Armstrong and Aldrin in what, he said, "certainly has to be the most historic telephone call ever made." The conversation was televised at both ends and shown on a split screen, with the President in his oval office at the White House, and the astronauts standing in front of their landing craft.

"Because of what you have done," the President said, "the heavens have become a part of man's world. And as you talk to us from the Sea of Tranquility, it requires us to redouble our efforts to bring peace and tranquility to earth. For one priceless moment in the whole history of man, all the people on this earth are truly one—one in their pride in what you have done and one in our prayers that you will return safely to earth."

Armstrong, the Apollo 11 commander, answered: "Thank you, Mr. President. It's a great honor and privilege for us to be here representing not only the United States but men of peace of all nations, men with interests and a curiosity and men with a vision for the future."

The astronauts wasted no time settling down to their chores. Each had a checklist printed on one sleeve of his moonsuit. Aside from sending back TV pictures and descriptions of the moon, they had two objectives: (1) to set out three scientific experiments; (2) to collect up to 60 pounds of lunar rocks and soil.

For the first experiment, Armstrong and Aldrin set up a sheet of aluminum foil a foot wide and a yard long for a solar-wind test. Its purpose was to trap rare outflowing gases from the sun— such as argon, krypton, xenon, neon, and helium. The aluminum foil with captured gases was placed in a vacuum box to be re-turned to earth for study. Scientists hoped this "wind" would throw light on the way in which the sun and planets were formed.

The second experiment was an instrument to report any

tremors caused by falling meteorites or volcanic eruptions. The reports, it was hoped, would provide clues to the makeup of the moon.

The third experiment, also left on the moon, was a 2-foot-square laser reflector made up of 100 fused-silica prisms. Pointed toward the earth, it was designed to reflect a beam of light directly back to the earth. By measuring the travel time of the pulses to the moon and back, scientists could use the reflector to trace very small changes in earth-moon distances. These changes might show whether gravity was weakening or the continents shifting, and might provide sensitive tests of scientific theories.

MINING THE MOON

Of all the experimental tasks, however, top priority went to the collection of rocks and soil. The samples taken by Armstrong and Aldrin, both amateur geologists with special training, were headed for the Lunar Receiving Laboratory in Houston for initial tests, and then, after a period of quarantine, to other laboratories across the country for more thorough study.

Armstrong scooped up the first "contingency" sample and put it in his pant-leg pocket almost as soon as he got out of the lunar module. This was even before Aldrin descended, and was done to assure having some lunar material if something suddenly went wrong on the surface and the astronauts had to "abort" the mission.

"Like it's a little difficult to dig through the crust," Armstrong said as he gathered up the sample. "It's very interesting. It's a very soft surface but here and there where I plug with the contingency sample collector, I run into very hard surface, but it appears to be very cohesive material of the same sort."

Later, while Aldrin was busy with other tasks, Armstrong

went farther from the module and collected more rocks and soil at random. Aldrin then took his turn, making more careful choices within a radius of up to 100 feet of the craft, while Armstrong took pictures. Since the spacesuits did not allow the astronauts to bend more than slightly, the men used scoops and tongs with long handles. This first lunar geological prospecting was seen very clearly on home TV screens. As the astronauts walked about, they described by radio what they saw. They put the samples in sealed aluminum boxes for the trip back to earth.

Here is how some of the conversation went:

Armstrong: Now this one's right down front. And I want to know if you can see an angular rock in the foreground.

Houston: Roger, we have a large angular rock in the foreground. And it looks like a much smaller rock a couple of inches to the left.

Armstrong: And beyond it about 10 feet is an even larger rock that's rounded. That rock is about—the closest one to you is about—that one sticking out of the sand—about one foot. It's about a foot and a half long and it's about six inches thick. But it's standing on edge.

Aldrin: Neil, I've got the table out . . . and the bag deployed.

Houston: Roger. And we see the shadow of the LEM.

Armstrong: The little hill just beyond the shadow of the LEM is a pair of elongated craters, so they appear together as 40 feet long and 20 feet across and they're probably six feet deep. We'll probably get more work in there later.

Houston: Roger. And we see Buzz going about his work.

Armstrong reported that he collected about 50 pounds of soil and rock samples from several areas within the limited excursion sector around the lunar module. Most of the samples he scooped off the surface, but he went as deep as three inches. There was no noticeable change in the soil at that depth. He did not hit any hard bed. Armstrong said there was a wide variety of rocks, and the boulders were generally about two feet high.

The rocks were coated with surface powder, making them slippery in the deep vacuum that exists on the lunar surface. Some of the rocks were full of cavities. Another rock was said to look like a biotite, a dark green or black form of mica that is found on rocks on earth.

As one of their last acts on the lunar surface, the moon men drove coring tubes into the surface with a hammer to capture deeper material that would be sure not to show any changes from the heat of the lunar module's landing rocket blast. Aldrin said he had no trouble going in about 2 or 3 inches, but then had to pound "about as hard as I could." He drove the tube about 8 or 9 inches into the surface, then he noticed something puzzling.

For some reason, he said, the tube "didn't seem to want to stand upright. I'd keep driving it in and it would dig some sort of a hole, but it wouldn't penetrate in a way that it would support itself." He added that the material in the tube was "quite well packed, a good bit darker and the way it adhered to the core tube gave me the distinct impression of being moist."

All in all, man's first walk on the moon lasted 2 hours and Armstrong and Aldrin climbed back up into the Eagle where they continued to radio their impressions to Houston before resting.

Armstrong and Aldrin still had the risky lift-off to rejoin the orbiting Columbia command ship which Colonel Collins had been piloting all this time. The two astronauts were completely dependent upon the 3,500-pound-thrust ascent rocket in the upper half of the lunar module. If it failed to fire, they would be stranded.

CHAPTER 13

Home
to Earth

Suspense on a space mission is always greatest when the ship is out of ground contact or is trying a maneuver for the first time. The suspense was never greater than on Monday, July 21, when Armstrong and Aldrin prepared to lift off the moon for the return home.

The ascent rocket in the upper half of the Lunar Module had been tested hundreds of times, of course; but never on the moon. And instead of a fully equipped launching pad for the lift-off, the astronauts had to trust the lunar module's lower half, which had been separated from the ascent stage by the firing of explosive bolts. At this point, the mission and the men's lives depended on these two pieces of equipment working perfectly.

But the engine fired on time and at full thrust. It lifted the ascent vehicle and sent it into a long orbital path toward a rendezvous with the waiting command ship. A sigh of relief went up at Mission Control in Houston as the lunar module radio reported: "Nine, eight, seven, six, five, first stage engine on ascent. Proceed. Beautiful. 26, 36 feet per second up. Little pitch over, very smooth, very quiet ride."

Four minutes later, the Eagle reported: "Eagle is back in orbit, having left Tranquility Base, and leaving behind a replica from our Apollo 11 patch with an olive branch."

That's not all the moon explorers left behind. On the site of the landing was the descent stage, no longer needed and therefore excess baggage. Around it, like the clutter left by some campers, were the cameras, walking boots, equipment boxes, an aluminum pole, two back packs and other equipment which the astronauts pitched out to lighten their load for take-off.

The lift-off came as Colonel Collins was piloting the command ship through its 25th revolution of the moon. Collins, who was somewhat of a forgotten man during the time his crewmates were performing their feats on the lunar surface, received an unofficial tribute from the space agency for doing the tasks usually shared by all three crewmen. The announcer at Mission Control said: "Not since Adam has any human known such solitude as Mike Collins is experiencing during the 47 minutes of each lunar revolution when he's behind the moon with no one to talk to except his tape recorder aboard Columbia."

Armstrong and Aldrin closed in for the rendezvous in a series of four maneuvers with the lunar module's smaller thruster jets. At about 69 miles above the front face of the moon, the Columbia joined its nose with the top hatch of the Eagle. As the two vehicles moved in for the link-up, their aim was off slightly; but the docking, though bumpy, was done without trouble.

Armstrong and Aldrin crawled through the connecting tunnel

to rejoin Collins, and then they jettisoned the lunar module, which became a piece of junk orbiting the moon. Finally, they fired the Apollo's main engine, boosting the craft out of lunar orbit for the 60-hour coasting voyage toward the splashdown in the Pacific.

ROUTINE TRIP BACK

The trip back was routine. Until the last few hours before splashdown, the astronauts had little work to do except for checking spacecraft systems, performing housekeeping chores, and conducting more television shows for the folks at home.

On one telecast Aldrin showed how easy it was to apply ham spread to a slice of bread, which he grabbed out of mid-air in the cabin. Collins took a playful drink by holding the water gun a few inches from his mouth and squirting the water in, much as a Spaniard drinking from a wineskin. Armstrong said: "No matter where you travel, it is nice to get home."

On another telecast the astronauts talked about what they had been through. Collins said, "This trip of ours to the moon may have looked simple and easy. I want to assure you that this has not been the case." He pointed out all the complex equipment involved, and talked about the thousands of workers "below the surface" who made the mission possible.

"We've come to the conclusion," Aldrin added, "that this has been far more than three men on a voyage to the moon, more still than the efforts of a government and industry team, more even than the efforts of one nation. We feel that this stands as a symbol of the insatiable curiosity of all mankind to explore the unknown."

It was on their trip back that the astronauts learned that the Soviet Union's unmanned spacecraft, Luna 15, which had held the world in suspense for more than a week, had apparently crashed into the moon's surface. Launched three days ahead of Apollo 11, Luna 15 was regarded by many observers as a Soviet rival to the American spacecraft. The Russians announced Tuesday morning that Luna 15 had "reached the moon's surface" and that its work had "ended." The fact that it went out of action as soon as it touched the lunar surface suggested that it was not a soft landing but a crash.

At 12:22 P.M. Thursday, the astronauts jettisoned the service module, the equipment section carrying the rocket engine, to start the final descent from 400,000 feet into the earth's atmosphere. When they reached the atmosphere, the earth's gravity was exerting such a pulling force that the capsule was traveling at more than 24,000 miles an hour. Then the earth's air gripped at the spacecraft, slowing its speed.

SAFELY HOME

Within minutes, the astronauts were in the water 950 miles southwest of Hawaii—home safe from man's first trip to the moon. The splashdown was one minute earlier than the time scheduled in the original flight plan. Waiting to welcome them aboard the recovery aircraft carrier, the U.S.S. Hornet, 11 miles away, was President Nixon. He was in the Pacific area en route to a tour of Asian countries.

"All three of us are excellent," the Apollo men radioed from their bobbing capsule. "Take your time."

The astronauts were given biological isolation garments by a frogman as soon as the hatch was open, as part of the quarantine program designed to avoid moon germs. And they were washed off when they climbed into a raft to await the recovery helicopter.

President Nixon watched the recovery proceedings from the Hornet's bridge, but he had to wait 55 minutes to talk with them after they reached the deck of the carrier. The helicopter that brought them was immediately towed to an elevator for lowering to the flight deck where the astronauts went into the mobile isolation trailer for a quick checkup.

When the meeting finally came, the smiling astronauts were peeking out a window of the van. Now wearing blue coveralls, the men appeared relaxed and happy as they jostled each other to look out the window. The President, with the band playing "Hail to the Chief," strode briskly down the carpet to the front of the van. He stood about three feet from the astronauts and spoke to them through a microphone-speaker hookup:

"Neil, Buzz, and Mike, I want you to know that I think I'm the luckiest man in the world, and I say this not only because I have the honor to be President of the United States, but particularly because I have the privilege of speaking for so many in welcoming you back to earth.

"I can tell you about all the messages we have received in Washington, over 100 foreign governments, emperors and presidents and prime ministers and kings, have sent the most warm messages that we've ever received.

"They represent over two billion people on this earth, all of them who have had the opportunity to see what you have done."

As throngs of sailors listened on the deck and millions of people watched on home television screens, Mr. Nixon then chatted with the astronauts about baseball, world news, the splashdown, and phone calls he made to their wives, "three of the greatest ladies," inviting them and the astronauts to a state dinner. In the middle of the banter, he suddenly blurted, "Gee, you look great! You feel as good as you look?"

"I feel just perfect, Mr. President," Armstrong, the Apollo commander, replied.

Then the President grew serious again:

"I was thinking as you know as you came down and we knew

it was a success and it had only been eight days—just a week, a long week—but this is the greatest week in the history of the world since the Creation. Because of what happened in this week, the world is bigger infinitely and also as I'm going to find in this trip around the world, and Secretary [of State William] Rogers will find as he covers the other countries in Asia, as a result of what you've done, the world's never been closer together before.

"And we just thank you for that, and I only hope that all of us in government, all of us in America, that as a result of what you've done we could do our job a little better, we can reach for the stars just as you have reached so far for the stars."

Armstrong, again answering for the crew, said: "We're just pleased to be back and very honored that you were so kind as to come out here and welcome us back, and we look forward to getting out of this quarantine and talking."

At the end of the short ceremony, the President waved to them and walked back to return to the deck. As he left, the astronauts waved out the window at the cheering sailors. Then they, too, turned into their isolation van to continue their quarantine.

The astronauts were scheduled to spend three days in the mobile trailer while it was shipped by the Hornet to Hawaii, thence by plane and truck to the Lunar Receiving Laboratory in Houston. There they were to remain in quarantine until August 11, going through post-flight debriefings. The 48 pounds of lunar rocks and soil they brought back were shipped immediately to the lab for study.

The completion of the great mission triggered celebrations across the nation, particularly at the control centers and at the homes of the astronauts' families. At Mission Control in Houston, the men stood up at their consoles, cheered, waved small American flags, and talked of flying men to Mars. On a small screen there appeared the Eagle emblem of the Apollo 11 and the words: "Task Accomplished. July 1969."

Man may now see the moon as a new world to explore or even colonize, a new frontier for his restless, curious mind. One long voyage ended will only begin a second. There will surely be many more landings on the moon, at different places for far longer times. There will eventually be laboratories orbiting the moon, giant telescopes peering at the heavens through clear, airless space, and domed villages on the surface.

Man may now see the moon as a steppingstone to the distant planets. It may become a place from which, because of its weak gravity, the more far-reaching expeditions of the future will be launched.

Man may now also see the moon and, knowing that he has been there, learn something about himself. He could gain a new sense of what is possible, a new confidence in himself. Considering that, in the 1960's, mankind suffered so many disappointments, a change in people's feelings may be the most important result of the Apollo voyage to the moon.

Is this too much to hope for?

To reach the moon, to see the earth as a small planet—that cannot help but have an impact on man's idea of himself and of what he can do. This is the hope and promise of man's first voyage to the moon.

CHAPTER 14

Moon
Treasure

Even before the three astronauts left their recovery ship, a small but precious cargo, the treasure of Apollo 11, was rushed to the Manned Spacecraft Center in Houston. The treasure was the rocks and soil Armstrong and Aldrin had scooped up from the moon's surface at Tranquility Base. The astronauts had packed and sealed the samples, which weighed about 48 pounds, in two air-tight aluminum containers each about the size of a small suitcase. The "rock boxes," as they were called, were transported separately from the ship to Ellington Air Force Base so that the whole shipment could not be lost in a single accident. About 24 hours after splashdown, the first box arrived at Ellington, where it was welcomed after the fashion of returning astronauts. Thomas O.

Paine, the NASA administrator, had personally escorted the box from the Hornet, and most of the high-level officials of the space center were standing on the tarmac as the giant jet cargo plane taxied to a stop. They saw to it that the box was safely transferred to a white panel truck with glass sides and then transported the five miles from Ellington to the Lunar Receiving Laboratory (LRL) for the beginning of months of painstaking scientific analysis.

Awaiting the moon samples were the 26 scientists who made up the preliminary examination team. They could hardly contain their jittery eagerness. "Scientifically, this will be worth more than any other material in history," said Elbert W. King, curator of the LRL.

On Saturday afternoon, July 26, scientists got their first look at the moon rocks. Four selected geologists—Clifford Frondel of Harvard University, Edward Chao of the United States Geological Survey, Robin Brett of the Manned Spacecraft Center, and King— watched the opening of the first box through a porthole in a vacuum chamber where conditions closely approximated those on the air-less moon. Jack Warren, an LRL technician, worked from outside the chamber. In this way, he was able to manipulate the box without contaminating it. While looking through a porthole, Warren inserted a needle through the box's wall to draw off and collect any gases that might have been given off by the rocks. Then he unlatched the lid, removed the upper layer of packing material, and lifted out a piece of aluminum foil that had been used to trap solar particles and the two lunar core samples. Finally, Warren removed the plastic-wrapped rocks with his gloved hands and cut open the top. "This moment," Brett said in his Australian accent, "is the beginning of the study of lunar rocks on earth. To earth scientists this is a very, very exciting time."

It was a tantalizing and frustrating experience, for the scientists found a coating of blackish, fine-grained dust made it impossible for them to determine immediately the nature or true color of the moon rocks. All Frondel could say was, "We have a box full of rocks coated by this layer of black material." Describing the way the dust seemed to stick to the rocks, Frondel said that he would like to "give them the good scrubbing they deserve."

In the days that followed, the laboratory technicians and geologists brushed the dust off the rocks and began to see what they had. The first box contained 20 rocks, weighing a total of about 17 pounds. The largest rock in the sample was estimated to be about seven inches long, five inches wide and two inches thick. The second box was opened August 4. It contained 31 pounds of fine-grained soil and rocks. Some rocks were as large as cobblestones and others as small as golf balls.

The scientists chipped some of the rocks to examine their interior structure. They studied fragments under a microscope, bombarded another small piece with electrons and X-rays. They picked and scraped, even vaporized a pinch of lunar dust at high temperatures. After the initial studies, they planned to take a rock apart almost atom by atom.

Man began to learn at last what the moon—the Sea of Tranquility at least—is made of. The initial examination of the first samples did not yield conclusive evidence to support or reject the theories of how the moon came to be what it is. Yet by piecing together the few hard bits of data that emerged and reading between the lines, a few tentative conclusions could be drawn:

The earth and the moon probably have common ancestries.

The two bodies are so much alike, geologically, that the relationship of the earth to the moon is more sisterly than maternal.

The chemistry of the moon rocks is unlike that of any known earth rocks. The moon rocks were surprisingly rich in titanium, chromium, and other elements with high melting points.

Vulcanism has been and still may be very much alive on

the moon. The earth's satellite probably is dotted with active volcanoes.

\# The moon, like the earth, has a surface crust and an interior that is molten or partly molten. The interior may consist of nickel or iron, as in the earth's core.

\# The lunar soil has been pulverized by thermal expansion and contraction through the tremendous temperature changes on the moon and by the impact of meteorites. The soil is interspersed with glassy material made by the vaporization and subsequently cooling of material struck by meteorites.

HOTTER THAN COLD?

The initial discovery about the moon rocks was neither surprising nor necessarily revealing. After their first good look, geologists were convinced that the rocks were igneous, which meant that they had solidified from molten material. This had been predicted by many lunar experts, and tended to confirm the remote-controlled chemical analysis made by the Surveyor spacecraft. Finding igneous rocks, instead of sedimentary rocks, seemed to eliminate the interesting but unlikely hypothesis that the moon's *maria* or plains, were sedimentary deposits from former oceans of water. But the discovery did not altogether settle the question of whether the moon is geologically "hot" or "cold," "dead" or "alive." Igneous rocks could be explained neatly by both schools of thought. Being igneous, the rocks may have been melted at some point in the moon's past by the heat generated in a collision with a large meteorite; in that case, the "impact" school of lunar scientists could support their claim that the moon is a cold, inactive body, lacking volcanic or other internal processes. But igneous rocks could also be the hardened lava that welled up from the moon's interior in a volcanic eruption; such a conclusion would support the "volcanic," or hot and alive, schools of lunar thinking.

When the geologists confirmed the presence of vesicles on some of the rocks, the weight of the evidence seemed to be tipped in favor of the "hot" school. Vesicles are the tiny holes formed as gases escaped, a promising sign of vulcanism. While he was on the moon, Armstrong remarked that he thought he saw vesicles. Later, when the geologists saw the vesicles for themselves, Brett referred to the discovery as the most important piece of information the astronauts had found on the moon.

Other data gave additional force to the "hot" school's contentions. Under microscopic examination, one of the lunar rocks and the fine dust was found to be a mixture of olivine, pyroxine and calcium-rich feldspar. Such a mixture is typical of what is found in igneous rocks that have come up to the surface of the earth from the deep interior; these are found, among other places, in the lava fields of Hawaii and along the Palisades across the Hudson River from New York City.

The seismometers left on the moon by the astronauts recorded and transmitted to earth more than a dozen "seismic events" in the first 10 days. Gary Latham of Columbia University and a team of other scientists believed that some of the recorded shock waves were caused by landslides, while other waves seemed to have resulted either from the impact of large meteorites or vulcanism. According to one theory, the landslides were movements of piles of lava that cooled in fragments, lost their cohesiveness and then slid downhill. Some seismic signals indicated the possibility of lunar landslides set off in crater walls by the drastic temperature changes causing contraction and expansion of the surface.

Whatever the origin of the shocks, recordings of their travels through the moon appear to have demonstrated that the moon is far more like the earth than many scientists had imagined. By studying the seismic patterns, Latham concluded that the moon, like the earth, is a multi-layered body with a crust and an interior core. This would indicate that the moon certainly was hot at some time in its history, and probably is still hot today. The earth's layering came about because its interior was sufficiently warmed by decaying radioactive material so that the heavy material sank to the core and the light material rose to form continents.

Eugene A. Shoemaker, lunar geologist from the California Institute of Technology and chief investigator for Apollo 11's geological results, concluded that the evidence "is overwhelming" to support the theory of lunar vulcanism. For, if the moon has had or still has a hot interior, it would also have known volcanic activity.

Harold C. Urey, the 76-year-old Nobel Prize chemist from the University of California at San Diego and a long-time advocate of the cold, dead moon, acknowledged that the lunar samples "look as though they could be lava flows." Said Urey: "I have thought for 20 years that we had a cold moon. I would say that on the basis of the present evidence . . . I shall certainly consider very carefully whether I should not revise that opinion."

It may turn out, as Walter Sullivan, the *Times* science editor, wrote, that "most of the lunar theories have some merit."

Most of those arguing a volcanic origin for many lunar features concede that the largest craters were formed by explosions, presumably from the impact of meteorites. This is evident, for example, in the bright "rays" that radiate from a number of them, apparently formed by debris thrown out at the time of the blast.

Some scientists are beginning to suspect that it is entirely possible that the moon is both hot and cold. "The moon," said Robert Jastrow, director of NASA's Goddard Institute for Space Studies in New York City, "has a warm heart and a cold exterior." In this view, developed by Jastrow, Paul Gast, a geochemist at Columbia University's Lamont Geological Observatory, and Robert Phinney, a geophysicist from Princeton University, the moon definitely has, or has had, a molten core; the igneous rocks are their evidence. But one problem stands in the way of full acceptance of the hot-moon idea. That is the presence, discovered by the Lunar Orbiters, of the moon's so-called mascons—the lump-like mass concentrations of material beneath the surface of the lunar seas.

In an article written for *The New York Times* after Apollo 11, Jastrow considered the mascon problem:

> If the interior of the moon is hot enough to produce the great floods of lava that cover the Sea of Tranquility, it should be sufficiently plastic to yield under the excess weight of the mascons, so that they will sink down into the interior and disappear, leaving no detectable gravitational effect. But they remain.

> I think that the answer to the puzzle lies in some theoretical studies of the variation of the temperature with depth within the moon. These studies suggest that if the moon is molten at all—and the materials contained in the Apollo 11 rock samples clearly indicate sources of molten material—then this material must come from deep within the moon's interior, perhaps 250 miles below the surface.

> According to these calculations, the outermost 250 miles of the moon form a relatively cold and strong shell of rock, thick enough to support the weight of the mascons without buckling or yielding.

> Underneath this thick, rigid shell is a molten or partly molten region, from which occasionally a finger or a sheet of molten rock forces its way to the surface, spreading over the lunar seas in a great, black flood of lava.

> This happens infrequently because the outer shell is so thick (earth's crust is a maximum of 25 miles thick), the best evidence being that lava last flooded the Sea of Tranquility

between 100 million and a few hundred million years ago. But because the forces of erosion are so weak on the moon, and surface is static and unchanging, the signs of this ancient volcanism are still preserved as if it had happened yesterday.

BEADS AND BUCKETSFUL OF SUN

Thus scientists who examined the first rocks from the moon were unable to come immediately to any fundamental conclusions about the earth's only natural satellite. They were, however, able to gain a wealth of information that should lead in time and with future exploration to a comprehensive picture of the lunar face and interior.

The biggest surprise from the initial examination of lunar soil was the abundance of tiny glass spheres, making up perhaps one-quarter to one-third of the samples studied. Columbia's Paul Gast called the tiny beads of glass "the most exciting" scientific discovery of the moon mission. The little spheres ranged in size from microscopic to a sand granule and were multicolored, from dark brown to yellow to clear. "The surprise is not in their existence," said Harvard's Clifford Frondel, "but in their abundance." As a "trial hypothesis," Frondel suggested that the glassy beads were formed when a meteorite smashed into the surface and generated such heat as to vaporize silica-rich lunar material. The glass probably condensed out of the vapor, solidified and rained on the moon.

That explanation raised a baffling question: Since lunar gravity is not even strong enough to retain an atmosphere, why did the vaporized material not drift off into space? There were no ready answers. The glass beads "have very interesting properties, a great deal of variety and they seem to be telling us that there is something going on on the moon that is a little bit different from what we had anticipated," Gast said.

More detailed observations led scientists to make a preliminary catalog of lunar elements. By burning a fragment of lunar soil and studying the different colors of its chemical elements in the flame, it was possible to identify 60 elements, from aluminum to manganese. The rocks appeared to be deficient in sodium and potassium, but rich in titanium; one lunar sample was assayed at 12 percent titanium, far more than found in any but the rarest earth rock. There were oxides of seven elements: silicon, aluminum, magnesium, sodium, calcium, iron and titanium.* "It would be very difficult to make an earth rock with this composition," said Ross Taylor, a New Zealand geochemist on the preliminary examination team at Houston. "The rocks are similar enough so that we can analyze them and refer them to terrestrial rocks. But in detail, the geochemistry is quite different. There are no current theories to explain this particular composition."

Another test indicated that the moon promises to be an excellent place to study the composition of the sun. When he heated a pinch of lunar dust to 3,000 degrees Fahrenheit, Oliver A. Schaeffer of the State University of New York at Stony Brook discovered in the escaping gases a surprisingly rich lode of the atomic particles that boil off the sun and, as the so-called solar wind, steadily bombard the moon's surface. Analysis showed that they were radioactive particles of helium, argon, neon, krypton and xenon. "We expected to find traces," Schaeffer said, "but we found bucketsful of solar wind."

In a similar test, Richard D. Johnson of NASA's Ames Re-

---

* The presence of titanium in the rocks could account for their purplish tint which Aldrin said he observed while on the moon. Armstrong was less sure of the so-called "purple rocks," and scientists at Houston came to suspect that the astronauts were pulling their legs.

search Center found the first possible evidence of organic compounds on the moon. Johnson reported finding less than 10 parts per million of such compounds, similar to those carbon compounds associated with living organisms on earth; this compared with perhaps 10,000 parts in a typical sample of earth soil. The minute quantity of the carbon content lead NASA scientists, Johnson included, to question whether the compounds were indigenous to the moon or had come from earthly contamination, possibly from the cabinets in which the samples had been placed.

Another chemist, William Schopf of the University of California at Los Angeles, placed lunar dust and rock chips under a 300,000-power microscope and could find no sign of lunar organisms, living, dead or fossilized. Scores of germ-free mice were exposed to the lunar samples—without any ill effect. This was particularly comforting news to Terry Slezak, a photographic technician at the LRL. When he inadvertently touched some moon dust on a film magazine brought back by Apollo 11, Slezak became the first man to touch lunar soil with his bare hands. He was promptly placed in quarantine—with the rocks and the astronauts —just in case he had brushed up against any lunar germs.*

GLASSY BOTTOMS AND WHITE HALOS

For all their mystery and value, the moon rocks were not an extraordinary sight. One expected them, almost wanted them, to be spectacularly different.

About two weeks after the rocks arrived at the LRL, I was

* Twenty-three people, including the astronauts, were placed in quarantine. They included doctors, technicians, a public information officer and those, like Slezak, who were accidentally exposed to lunar samples. One young woman, a laboratory technician working with the experimental mice, had to enter quarantine when she became exposed. All of them, pronounced free of any lunar contamination, were released August 10.

among a dozen newsmen who gathered in a viewing room at the laboratory for the public's first look at one of the moon rocks. There it was, in lonely splendor behind the plate glass window, a small gray rock flecked with tiny crystals and bearing a faint tint of pinkish brown. The two-pound rock, about three inches long and 1½ inches thick, was enclosed in a glass vacuum jar.

Jeffrey L. Warner, an LRL geologist, pointed out the many tiny pits in the rock. Under a microscope, he explained, most of the pits were seen to have black glassy bottoms with white halos. This indicated that long after the rock was formed it was bombarded by high-velocity particles, probably micrometeorites or fragments sent flying by impacts elsewhere on the moon. The white rings, Warner said, suggested that the heat generated by the impacts produced additional crystallization.

The texture of the rock's grains were described as being "like sugar." Like most of the others, it consisted of elements in the families of minerals known as olivine, pyroxene and feldspar, similar to rocks Warner, a native New Yorker, said he had often picked up in the Hudson Palisades. But it was not a simple rock. It settled no scientific arguments over the moon's origin, its cratered surface or its interior. It and the other rocks would give 142 scientists, the principal investigators, months of challenging work. "This rock," Warner commented, "tells us that the history of the moon is very complicated."

Index